THE STORY
OF THE INDIAN

BY

GEORGE BIRD GRINNELL

AUTHOR OF PAWNEE HERO STORIES AND FOLK TALES,
BLACKFOOT LODGE TALES, ETC.

ILLUSTRATED

NEW YORK
D. APPLETON AND COMPANY
1902

Copyright, 1895,
By D. Appleton and Company.

THE STORY OF THE INDIAN

By George Bird Grinnell
Originally Published in 1902

©2001 DSI digital reproduction
First DSI Printing: January 2001

Published by **DIGITAL SCANNING, INC.**
Scituate, MA 02066
www.digitalscanning.com

All rights reserved, which includes the right to reproduce this book or portions thereof in any form whatsoever except as provided by the U.S. Copyright Law. For information address Digital Scanning, Inc.

Trade Paperback ISBN: 1-58218-245-0
Hardcover ISBN: 1-58218-246-9
eBook ISBN: 1-58218-244-2

DIGITAL SCANNING
& PUBLISHING

Digital Scanning and Publishing is a leader in the electronic republication of historical books and documents. We publish our titles as eBooks, as well as traditional hardcover and trade paper editions. DSI is committed to bringing many traditional and little known books back to life, retaining the look and feel of the original work.

The Distant Camp

EDITOR'S NOTE.

THE books which are to appear in this series are intended to present peculiar and characteristic phases of earlier development in that portion of our country which lies beyond the Missouri River. The specialization of American history has found expression in numerous studies of the colonial life of New England, New York, and Virginia, indeed, all the Eastern seaboard, and in discussions of explorations westward like those of the Spaniards to the south and the French to the north, and of migrations away from the seaboard, like the movement across the Blue Ridge to Kentucky, and the various patriarchal journeyings which began the settlement of Ohio and the middle West. The final occupation of the real West has come about almost in our own time. The first white male child born in Kansas is an honoured resident of the State to-day, and Kansas is venerable in comparison with States and Territories beyond. Speaking roughly, the Missouri divides sections very dissimilar in certain characteristics of their evolution. It is not a question of political differences, like those which have sundered Kansas and Missouri, but of differences due to the strength of the Indian holding, the character of a soil fitted throughout vast areas for grazing rather than cultivation, and the presence of stores of treasure in

two mighty mountain systems, which have drawn into
their recesses the trapper and the hunter as well as
the prospector. For our real West, therefore, the
typical figures are the Indian, the explorer, the soldier, the miner, the ranchman, the trapper, if we take
into consideration the northern fur trade, and the
railroad builder. The representative explorer may be
found in Lewis and Clarke, or Pike or Fremont, or
that more remote and romantic Argonaut, Coronado.
The soldier has never received a tithe of justice for
the heroism of his lonely and perilous service on the
plains. The miner's kaleidoscopic career, ranging
from the grub-staked prospector to the millionaire
gambling on the stock exchange with loaded dice, has
been too obvious to be neglected in the past, and the
complete story, as illustrated "on the Comstock," will
be unfolded by Mr. Shinn. With these figures the
West has offered us the cowboy, that most individual
and picturesque of types, and, following the soldier
and oftentimes preceding settlement, the railroad
builder. The latter's perilous reconnaissances, stormy
life in the construction camps, and warfare with
Indians, thugs, and sometimes with rival builders,
deserve well of the historian who cares for human interest and not merely for the engineering difficulties
overcome, and the financial results. There are other
types, like the one afforded by the noble figure of
Father Junipero Serra and by the hunter, the pony
express rider, the road agent, and later the men of
the wheat and fruit ranches, and the irrigating
ditch, and those curious children of Ishmael, the
"boomer" and "sooner." But if we take the phases
typified in the figures which I have emphasized it
is plain that the series of pictures will be individ-

ual, racy of the Western soil in the truest sense, and also of permanent historical value, since they will preserve in definite form these picturesque and original aspects of Western development of which we are apt to catch only distorted and fleeting glimpses. This is the object of a series planned through the editor's knowledge of the real West, a knowledge gained by actual experiences of ranch and mining and Indian life between Sonora and Vancouver and Texas and Dakota, and also through a love for the types illustrated, a desire to record their characteristics before they have entirely vanished and a hearty belief in what I may term their pictorial value for the historian.

There is no word simpler and more elastic than the word story to describe the plan of the series, and although we shall deal with the realities of history, the humbler term seems more broadly significant. These books are intended to be stories of human interest, not categories of facts. Mr. Grinnell, for example, might have written a history of the Indian tribes west of the Missouri, which would have been only a valuable repository of facts. But, instead of this, Mr. Grinnell takes us directly to the camp fire and the council. He shows us the Indian as a man subject to like passions and infirmities with ourselves. He shows us how the Indian wooed and fought, how he hunted and prayed, how he ate and slept—in short, we are admitted to the real life of the red man, and as we learn to know him we discard two familiar images: the red man of the would-be philanthropic sentimentalist, and the raw-head-and-bloody-bones figure that has whooped through so many pages of fiction. A typical explorer and a typical mine will be the subjects of volumes closely following this. In each case the effort will be to embody the essential features of the general theme in one descriptive history with one central point of interest, thus forming a series free from cumbersome details, but breathing the spirit and preserving the qualities of reality. Since the subjects form a part of our history they will be treated with a view to the historical student's demand for exactness of statement and soundness of inference, and since these stories illustrate a most romantic phase of our past, the elements of colour and atmosphere and quick human interest are inseparable from the treatment. Either older or younger readers who care to live over again certain wholly individual phases of our country's history may, it is hoped, draw from these volumes some such sense of the reality of romantic history as Parkman has left us in his pictures of the earlier phases of Canadian life and history, in his Oregon Trail and his Discovery of the Great West.

INTRODUCTION.

THIS volume might be called one of recollections, for in it have been set down many memories of Indian life. The scenes described I have witnessed with my own eyes; the stories related are those which have been told me by the Indians themselves.

These stories are introduced freely because the concrete example conveys a clearer idea of an event than an abstract statement, and because the story of the Indian should not be told wholly from the point of view of a race alien in thought, feeling, and culture. No narrative about any people can do them justice if written by one who is not in some degree in sympathy with them, and acquainted with their ways of thought and with the motives which govern them. Before an intelligent account of it can be given, the stranger race must be comprehended. Long association with Indians enables a white man ultimately to share their thought and feelings; and he who has reached this point understands the Indian. He understands that the red man is a savage and has savage qualities, yet he sees also that the most impressive characteristic of the Indian is his humanity. For in his simplicity, his vanity, his sensitiveness to ridicule, his desire for revenge, and his fear of the supernatural, he is a child and acts like one.

We are too apt to forget that these people are human like ourselves; that they are fathers and mothers, husbands and wives, brothers and sisters; men and women with emotions and passions like our own, even though these feelings are not well regulated and directed in the calm, smoothly flowing channels of civilized life. Not until we recognise this common humanity may we attain the broader view and the wider sympathy which shall give us a true comprehension of the character of the Indian.

The present volume professes to give only a general view of Indian life, and many interesting topics have necessarily been referred to only incidentally. In the stories given I have followed the language of the interpreters through whom I received their narratives directly from the Indians.

Mr. James Mooney, of the Bureau of Ethnology, has very kindly read the chapter on the North Americans, on which he made a number of valuable suggestions, and for which he furnished most of the translations of the tribal names. My friend Mr. Charles B. Reynolds has read over the whole manuscript, and the form of the book owes much to his kindly criticisms. To both these gentlemen my acknowledgements are due.

CONTENTS.

xi

LIST OF ILLUSTRATIONS.

THE STORY OF THE INDIAN.

CHAPTER I.

HIS HOME.

YELLOW under the burning sun lies the far-stretching prairie. In one direction the rounded swells rise and fall like the heaving breast of ocean after a storm has passed; in another, the ragged ravine-seamed soil rears sharp crests like billows tossed by the storm in fury. In the distance the level sweep of the horizon is broken by high buttes, some square-topped and vertical-sided, others slender and sharp-pointed—like huge fortresses or cathedral spires. All are dotted here and there with gnarled, stunted black pines and cedars, that, with tenacious grip, cling to the bare rocks from which they draw a sustenance—scanty, yet sufficient.

Scattered over the prairie far and near are the wild denizens of this land: brown buffalo feeding or resting, yellow antelope singly or in groups, a family of wolves playing at the mouth of a ravine, prairie dogs in their towns, little birds swinging on the tops of the sage bushes, and over all a blue arch in which swings motionless a broad-winged eagle.

Away to the westward, so far that the forest-clad

foothills are purple with distance and the rough rock slopes gray with haze, stands the mighty wall of the Continental Divide. White and grey and brown, snow fields and rock peaks, and high naked plateaus rear rough outlines against the blue of the summer sky, or are blotted out mile by mile when black storm clouds creep down from the peaks toward the plains, which the summer storms never reach.

This is the country of the Indian of the West.

Here the prairie is split by a great crooked gash—a river's course—to which the ravines all run. Down in the valley the silvery leaves of cottonwood tremble, copses of willow and bits of fresh growing grass stand along the stream, and there is the shimmer of flowing water, coolness, and shade. This is the Indian's home.

The cone-shaped dwellings stand in a rough circle which touches the river bank. Some of the lodges are newly made, clean, and white; others are patched, grey with weather stain, and smoke browned near the top. Each conical home terminates in a sheaf of crossing lodge poles, and between the extended "ears" shows a wide dark opening from which rise curling wreaths of blue smoke. Some of the lodges are painted in gay colours with odd angular figures of men, and animals, and guns, and camp fires, which tell in red, black, or green of the *coups* of the owner—his brave deeds or strange adventures. Here and there from the lodge poles of some leading man hangs a buffalo tail, or one or two eagle feathers are turning in the breeze, or a string of little hoof sheaths, which rattle as they are shaken in the wind, runs from the lodge poles nearly to the ground.

Leaning against the lodges, and, if standing on end, quite equalling the lodge poles in height, are the travois, the universal vehicle. Before or behind the lodges of medicine men, chiefs, and noted braves hang the medicine bundles of the doctors and priests, and the arms and war dresses of the warriors. Tripods of slender poles support the sacks or bundles, or sometimes a lance is thrust in the ground, and to it is tied the warrior's equipment. The eagle feathers, scalps, and fringes with which these things are ornamented, wave gaily in the breeze.

Near the stream bank, above and below the camp, stand curious low frames, woven of willow branches, and looking somewhat like large bird cages of wickerwork. Some are oval and others hemispherical, and in the ground which forms their floor a little hollow is dug out in the centre, in which are ashes and a number of stones which show the marks of fire. Besides this, on the ground outside each one, is a spot where a little fire has been built, and near the fireplace are other round stones. These are the sweat lodges of the camp, where are taken the steam baths used in healing and in certain religious rites.

Up and down the stream valley, and scattered over the bordering bluffs, are the horses, for the most part wandering at will, though here and there a group is herded by a boy or young man who spends most of his time lying on the ground in the shade of his horse, but now and then clambers on its back and gathers together his little band or drives away others that seem disposed to mingle with it. There are hundreds—perhaps thousands—of horses in sight, dotting the valley, the bluffs, and even the distant upper plains.

Here and there on little elevations, on the points of the bluffs or on the river bank—usually on some commanding eminence—are single figures of men. Closely wrapped in his robe or his summer sheet, each one remains apart from all the others, and sits or stands for hours motionless. These men have left the camp and retired to such places to be alone. Some of them are praying; some are acting as sentries, looking over the country to see if enemies are approaching; some desire to think out their projects without fear of interruption; while it is possible that among the motionless figures may be one who belongs to some hostile tribe and has ventured thus boldly to expose himself in order to learn the ways of the camp, to find out how the watchers are disposed, where the swiftest horses are kept, at what points an attack may be made with best prospects of success. If such a spy is here, he is for the present safe from detection. He feels sure that no one will approach him or speak to him, for when a man goes off in this way by himself it is understood by all that he wishes to be alone, and this wish is respected.

Within the circle of the camp the daily life of the people is going on. Moving forms, clad in bright colours, pass to and fro, and people are clustered in the shade of the lodges. Tied near most of the doors are one or two horses for immediate use. Now and then the bark of a dog falls upon the ear, and above the indistinct hum of camp life are heard the whoops or shrieks of children at play.

Everywhere groups of men are seated in the shade, smoking, chatting, or sleeping. Some are naked, some clad only in a blanket, but most wear leggings of deer or cow skin and are wrapped in sheets of dressed cow skin. Here with infinite care a young dandy is painting himself; there a man is sharpening arrowheads;

a third is mending a saddle; another fashioning a pipe stem.

Without the circle of the camp, off toward the bluff, stands a group of men, some of them naked to the breech-clout, others, spectators, wrapped in their sheets or blankets. At intervals two naked men are seen to dart out from this group and race along, near-ly side by side, throwing their sticks at some object that rolls along in front of them. Often at the end of such a race there is a loud-voiced dispute as to which contestant has won, in which the two racers and their friends take part with violent gesticulations and earnest speech. This is the stick or wheel game.

Down by one of the sweat lodges a woman is kin-dling fires and heating the stones in the centre of the lodge and outside. She covers the frame with robes or skins, so as to keep the heat in. A bucket of water stands near the fire. Soon half a dozen young men come to the place, and, following them, an older man who carries a pipe. As they reach the lodge, they drop their blankets and creep naked beneath the cov-ering. After a little the old man is heard singing his sacred songs and in monotonous voice praying for the success of those who are about to start on a journey which will be full of danger. The woman passes a vessel into the sweat house; the water hisses as it falls on the hot stones, and steam creeps forth from the crevices in the covering. Then there is more singing, and other low-voiced mumbling, prayers in different voices, and at length after an hour, the coverings of the lodge are thrown off, the men creep out, rise, and, all wet with perspiration and bleeding where they have cut themselves in sacrifice, file down to the stream and plunge into its cold waters. This is the medicine sweat, and the young men who have taken part in it are about to start off on the warpath.

All day long the women who have remained in camp have been at work tanning hides, sewing lodges, making dried meat, and pounding pemmican, and they are still busy, though soon these tasks will be laid aside for the day. As yet they are still bent double over the green hides, chipping at them with fleshers, and now and then raising themselves for a moment's rest, and with one hand brushing away the overhanging hair from their foreheads, while with hands on hips they bend back to stretch themselves and ease their muscles. In the shade of the lodges sit other women, with stone hammers pounding choke cherries on flat stones. The tasks are not performed in silence. The little groups that work near to one another keep up a lively fire of gossip and jest which give rise to abundant merriment. A woman who has an established reputation for wit is telling with monotonous unchanging voice and without a particle of expression in her face a story that overwhelms her sisters with mirth. They cackle forth shrill laughter, and exchange delighted comment, but the story goes on without interruption.

The women wear sleeveless leather gowns reaching to below the knees and belted at the waist, and from this belt dangle by small chains or leather thongs the knife, fire steel, and sewing bag, which are a part of each one's equipment. The gowns of the older women are often old and worn, patched here and there, and black with blood, grease, and dirt. The clothing of the younger ones, the daughters or wives of men well to do, is handsome, being clean, tanned very white, heavily beaded and ornamented

Pawnee Woman Dressing a Hide

with elk tushes, trimmed with red and blue cloth, and fringed at the edges. As a rule, the younger women are better dressed and much more careful of their personal appearance than those older, though sometimes the latter are neat and give some attention to their hair.

But for the women it is not all hard work. Here and there groups are to be seen sewing moccasins or fashioning for husband or children buckskin leggings, shirts, or other apparel, or ornamenting such clothing with beadwork or with beautifully stained quills of the porcupine. In these tasks much taste is displayed, savage though it be. Besides these workers, there are not a few who are tempting fortune. In some cool spot two lines of women sit opposite each other, and behind each person, or at her side, is a little pile of her possessions which she is betting on the seed game, played with plum stones and a little flat basket.

Scattered about through the camp, up and down the stream and on the open ground nearly to the bluffs, are the children of these mothers. The tiniest of them—those who have been facing the fierce prairie sun only for a few weeks or months—are securely tied to their boards—the primitive cradle—from which they gaze solemnly with unwinking eyes on this new and uncomprehended world. The boards are hung up on poles or drying scaffolds or travois, or lean against a lodge, a sage bush, or even a buffalo skull, and no attention is paid to their occupants, save now and then when they whimper and have to be nursed. Other children, a little older, have been freed from this imprisonment, and with a bit of dried or fresh meat in their hands grovel on the ground, alternately chewing at the meat and rubbing it in the dust until their faces are plentifully caked with mud. Some have already tired of their unaccustomed freedom, and cry piteously to be put back on their boards, ceasing their lamentations as soon as preparations are made to confine them again.

The children old enough to walk are comical to look at, though rather troublesome to live with. The girls are mostly clad in little smocks which reach to their bare knees, but not so much can be said for the clothing of the boys. Some of them have a string tied about the waist, and some pet of his father or grandfather may have a buckskin string about his neck which carries a few beads or an amulet to keep off disease or the ghosts. Usually, however, they run about clad only in their close-fitting brown hides, which gather only a moderate amount of dirt, and which, when they tear, do not have to be mended.

Coming from the direction of a large lodge and walking with downcast eyes across the circle of the camp, passes a young girl bearing in her hand a covered wooden dish. She is beautifully clad in a dress of white skins, beaded, fringed, trimmed with red cloth and ornamented with elk tushes. Her hair is shining and neatly braided behind each ear, and the paint on her face and in the parting of the hair is bright and fresh. Closely following her, walks another young girl, and after they have crossed the circle they enter a lodge, which, by its size and ornamentation and by the arms and medicine bundles which stand near it, is evidently that of an important man—some chief. The girl who carries the food is betrothed to the son of the owner of the lodge which she enters, for now—during the time between the arrangement for the marriage and its consummation—she serves her future lord with food each day, making the journey from her father's lodge to his, accompanied only by a sister or young girl friend.

As the sun falls toward the western horizon the aspect of the camp begins to change; there is more activity, more people are moving about. The women begin to put aside the work of dressing hides, to kindle their fires anew, and to go to the stream for water. From up and down the creek and from over the bluff, single figures and small groups of people are approaching the camp. Some of these are women who have made long journeys to secure a supply of wood, which they bring home on their backs or piled high on the dog travois. Most of those who are coming in are men who have been off hunting on the plains, killing food. The camp is in a buffalo country and there has been a general chase. The circle of the lodges has been almost deserted during the early part of the day, for men and women alike have been off to the hunt, the men to do the killing and the women to bring the meat and hides to camp. The last of these are now returning in little groups, and almost every one is perched on top of the load of dripping meat borne by the horse she rides, and leading one or two pack horses still more heavily laden.

All through the day more or less feasting has been going on, but this takes place chiefly toward evening. One who desires to entertain his friends has directed his wife to prepare the food for his guests, and when all is ready either sends a messenger about through the camp to invite them, or has him loudly shout out their names from his own lodge door. But little time elapses before the guests begin to arrive, and one by one to enter the lodge. Each is welcomed by the usual salutation and his seat is indicated to him, the more important men being seated furthest back in the lodge and nearest to the host's left hand. After a prayer and the sacrifice of a portion of the food, the eating begins without much waste of words. The portion set before each man is all he is to receive, he will not be helped a second time. Among some tribes it is not good manners for a guest to leave any food on the dish set before him, but among others, if the man does not care to eat it all, he may carry away with him that which is left. Usually the host does not eat with his guests. While they are disposing of their food, he is cutting up and mixing the tobacco for the smokes which are to follow. As the eating draws to a close, conversation begins, and at length the host, having filled the pipe, passes it to a son or a servant on his right, who lights and then returns it. The host makes the ceremonial smokes—to the sky, to the earth, and to the four cardinal points—prays and then hands the stem to his left hand neighbor, who, after smoking and praying, passes it to the man next him, and so it goes from hand to hand round the circle. It is during this smoking that the formal speech-making—if there is any—takes place. The subjects touched on are as various as the speakers, and it is noticeable that each one is listened to with patience and courtesy, and is never interrupted. He finishes what he has to say before another man begins to speak. About a lodge where a feast is going on, a number of uninvited people gather to listen to these speeches, and now—for it is summer and the lodge skins are raised for air—such listeners sitting about on the ground are in full view of the feasters. No one recognises any impropriety in such an outside gathering. If the number of guests at a feast be small,

all the men sit at the right of the door—on the host's left—and the family, the women and children, are on the left of the door, in that place in the lodge which belongs to them; but if the number of guests is large, the family moves out of the lodge for the time being.

As twilight falls the herds of horses from the bluffs and the upper prairie come trooping close to the camp, driven by the small boys and young men whose duty it is to attend to this. The most valuable, the swiftest, are tied to pins driven in the ground close to the lodge door, and the others are allowed to go free and soon work back to the hills near at hand. A man who has one or more running horses that he greatly values, perhaps confines them in a tight pen of logs and poles, lashed together with thongs of rawhide.

As darkness settles down over the camp, the noise increases. The shrill laughter of the women is heard from every side, partly drowned now and then by the ever-recurring feast shout. From different quarters comes the sound of drumming and singing, here from a lodge where some musicians are beating on a parfleche and singing for a dance, there where a doctor is singing and drumming over a sick child. Boys and young men are racing about among the lodges, chasing each other, wrestling, and yelling. In front of some lodge in the full light of the fire which streams from the open doorway, stand two forms wrapped in a single robe—two lovers, whispering to each other their affection and their hopes. Dogs bark, horses whinny, people call to each other from different parts of the camp. The fires shine through lodge skins and showers of sparks float through the smokeholes. As the night wears on the noises become less. One by one the fires go out and the lodges grow dark. From those where dancing is going on or a party of gamblers are playing the noise and light still come, but at last even these signs of life disappear, the men disperse, and the silence of the camp is broken only by the occasional stamp of an uneasy hoof or the sharp bark of a wakeful dog.

No incident mars the quiet of the night. The moon rises and under its rays the aspect of the circle is changed. All the camp is flooded with the clear light, interrupted only where the lodges cast their long shadows, or the ground is marked with slender lines fallen from the drying scaffolds, or from the tripods which support the arms or the medicine bundles. Before each lodge stand one or two horses, visible now only as dusky shapes, silent and motionless. The brilliant light of the moon, which shows so clearly objects near at hand, makes those a little further off vague and indistinct, as if seen through a mist, and in the distance the lodges of the circle fade out of sight.

Close at hand is a lodge larger than those near to it, and shining white and new in the moonlight. On the cow skins are drawn many pictures which tell the history of its owner, and before the door are tied four horses, his swiftest and best. This is the lodge of Three Suns, the chief, and on either side of it, for some distance around the circle, stand those of his immediate following, who are also his kinsmen.

The night wears on, and as the day approaches the first faint sounds of life begin to be heard. Now and then faintly upon the listening ear falls the distant whistle of the wild ducks' wings as a flock of birds start on their early morning flight up the stream. From a hill near the camp come the sharp barks and dolorous wails of the coyotes, answered from different points in the camp by the voices of half a dozen alert dogs. The tied horses, which have been lying down, rise to their feet and shake themselves, and the low whinny of a mare is responded to by a shrill call from the little colt near by.

In Three Suns' lodge all is quiet as yet; only the heavy regular breathing of the sleepers ranged about the walls shows that there is life there. Here and there, through some crevice between the lodge skins, a tiny thread of moonlight pierces the gloom, rendering the blackness within more intense. Only above through the wide smoke-hole is there any suggestion of light, where the sinking moon still illuminates one of the ears, and below, in the centre of the floor, a dim circle of white ashes tells where the daily fire burns.

As the night grows older and the moon sets and the eastern sky begins to pale, there is movement in the lodge, a restless turning in the side where the women sleep, and the querulous voice of a disturbed child is heard. One of the women throws aside her robe, and, rising, steps to the door and looks out; then, turning, she takes from under one of the beds some tinder, dried grass, and slivers of dry wood prepared the night before. With a stick she rakes aside the ashes, looking for a live coal, but, failing to find one, uses her flint and steel, and strikes a shower of sparks which kindle the dry fungus. The punk is placed in the dried grass, a little blowing starts a flame, and soon the lodge is brightened by a flickering fire, and sparks begin to fly out of the smokehole. By this time two other women have risen from their conches, and while one looks after the awakening children, the other goes down to the stream for water.

In the gray light, which, constantly growing brighter, now shows the whole camp, pillars of blue smoke rise from every lodge straight upward through the still cool air. Many women are hurrying to the stream for water; young men, close wrapped in their robes, are loosening the horses which have been tied up during the night, and they walk briskly off toward the hills. There is more or less noise and bustle— the chattering of women; the shrill calls of colts that have lost their mothers; the yell of pain from some dog that during the night has crept into a lodge to sleep warm with the children and is now discovered and driven out with blows. All these are the sounds of the awakening day.

The tops of the bluffs along the river are just beginning to be touched with yellow light as the door of Three Suns' lodge is pushed aside, and the chief himself comes out. His robe hides all his person but the head and the naked feet. His face is kindly and dignified, and he talks pleasantly to the little boy of three or four years whom he carries in his arms and whose head shows above the robe beside his father's. Darting about, before and behind or by the side of the father, is another son, a lad of twelve, naked as at birth, and holding in his hand a bow and several arrows, which as he races along he discharges at various marks that present themselves—the blackbirds swinging from the tops of the sage brush, the ground squirrels which scuttle from under the tufts of grass, or even the stones which lie on the prairie.

From other lodges come other men and boys, all like Three Suns and his children, walking toward the river. When it is reached they drop their robes, and all plunge in, the fathers taking even the smallest children and dipping them beneath the water, from which they emerge squirming and kicking but silent. The older boys dash into the water, and are riotously splashing about, shouting, and diving. Soon all again have sought the bank, and the men, donning their robes, return to the lodges. Here the pots have been boiling for some time, and when Three Suns has put on his leggings and moccasins, combed out his long hair, and again belted his robe about him, his first wife sets before him a horn platter, on which are some choice pieces of buffalo meat. Then the children are served, and the women help themselves; and when all have eaten, the men start off to hunt, the women set about their daily work in the camp, and the children disperse to their play.

So goes the round of Indian life. Another day has begun.

CHAPTER II.

Iт is a clear, bright morning. The horizon's out-line is sharply defined against the sky's unbroken blue, and the shadows are growing shorter as the sun climbs higher. The first meal has been eaten. The men have gone about their daily pursuits, and now only the last of the hunting parties may yet be seen, some riding off down the valley and others climbing the bluffs. Many men are in the camp, because the buffalo are not near by; but other animals which people eat, and whose skins are good for clothing, are plenty not far away—antelope on the prairies, deer and elk in the wooded ravines and river bottoms, and sheep on the buttes and rough bad lands.

In the camp the daily life goes on. White-haired old men, holding their robes as close about them as if it were winter, crouch, two or three together, by the lodges, and hold slow-voiced converse with one an-other; young men are sitting in the bright sun braid-ing their hair and painting their faces; women are tanning hides, or making dried meat, or pounding pemmican. Close by some of the old men, sit groups of boys, eagerly listening to the talk; and most of the women have—on their backs or hung up near to them —stolid fat brown babies. Dogs lie curled up in the

16

sun, and horses stand before the lodges with heads held low and drooping ears.

Of the home-staying folk the children form the most active and most noisy groups. They are everywhere, and the sound of their voices is heard continually. They run, play, shout, and effervesce with life and spirits, like youth the world over.

Like other young animals, these children delight to do the things which occupy their elders. So you will see each one engaged in some task or sport which represents the pursuits of the adults. All the older boys are armed with bows and headless arrows, and practice continually shooting at a mark or for distance, or sending the arrow almost vertically into the air in the effort to make it fall at some particular point. They hunt ground squirrels, blackbirds, and even prairie chickens and hares, and, during the season of migration, lie in wait by the streams and pools for ducks and geese. Some who have not yet reached the age at which they can effectively use the bow, drag about after them ropes or strings, and try to lasso each other or the unlucky dogs, trotting here and there among the lodges. A set younger still give themselves up to the delights of tormenting the dogs, and armed with pieces of wood as heavy as they can wield, take pleasure in stealing up to a dog slumbering in the shade and pounding the poor brute, which yells dismally, and at once betakes himself to some more secure resting place.

Others of the young braves are engaged in sham battles. Small parties conceal themselves behind neighbouring lodges and conduct a mimic fight much after the manner of men. As arrows, even though headless, would be dangerous in this pretended warfare, the opposing forces are armed with limber switches, and carry under the left arm a lump of wet clay. A bit of clay is pressed on the small end of the switch and thrown as a missile, just as the white boy throws a green apple with like implement. When the fight begins, a member of one party sallies out from behind his shelter and runs toward the enemy, throwing his mud balls at those who are peeping out at him. Before he has advanced very far two of the opposing party rush out and attack him. He retreats, is re-enforced by others from his own side and drives back the enemy, who in turn are strengthened from their own party. There are alarums and excursions, yells of defiance, cries of terror, shouts of fury and excitement from all the small warriors, a plentiful shower of mud balls, and finally each party retreats to shelter for rest and the renewing of ammunition. Such battles are interesting to watch between parties of footmen, but when two or three combatants on horseback are set upon by a number unmounted, the excitement is much greater. The mounted men charge upon the footmen, who fly to their shelter, throwing back as they run a cloud of mud balls, before which the cavalry retreat to a safe distance. Then a few of the footmen steal from their cover, trying to get within range, yet not venturing so far that they will be overtaken in the event of a charge. Very likely the mounted forces retire to decoy their assailants still further away; but at length they charge, then there is a helter-skelter retreat, re-enforcements rush forth, and the yelling and excitement are worthy of a real battle. So the fight will go on for half a day, one of either party now and then having a *coup* counted on him or being captured.

From the river which runs by the camp comes a

babble of childish voices, interrupted now and then
by piercing yells and sounds of splashing in the water.
A group of boys are diving, swimming, and wrestling
in a pool, as nimble and as much at home in the water
as so many fishes; and near by on the bank two or
three lads, who have come from the water, are sitting
naked in the sun, slowly and laboriously fashioning
figures of clay, which they carefully support against
the bank to dry. The images represent horses, dogs,
buffalo, and men, and though rude and often grotesque, may sometimes be recognised. To make them
is a favourite amusement of the children.

If the boy at his play rehearses the warlike pursuits
of the years to come, not less do the little girls share
the cares and duties of womanhood. Close by a lodge
several are at play tending their dolls. The largest,
who may be ten years old, is fashioning a pair of tiny
moccasins from some bits of dressed antelope skin.
These may be for the baby she carries on her back—
a puppy—whose sharp eager eyes, excited yelps, and
occasional ineffectual struggles show that he is not
altogether contented with his place upon the child's
shoulders. At each effort her play baby makes to get
free, the girl hitches up her blanket and draws it closer
about her, speaking sharply to him as a woman would
speak to an unruly child. Other little girls are busy
with dolls made of rolls of buckskin, with a head
rudely painted in black on one end. Some of them
are lashed to boards in the usual way, but one has
been freed from its confinement and is held in the
arms. This one has, tied to the end of its buckskin
arm, a bit of dried meat, which its nurse holds to its
mouth from time to time, as if to keep it quiet. The
dolls are nursed and looked after much as a parent

3

would treat a baby. The little girls play at feeding them, sing to them the same plaintive, monotonous songs their own mothers have used to hush them to sleep, take them down to the stream to wash them, and sew for them tiny moccasins and other clothing.

On the stream bank not far from the camp a group of girls are busy about two tiny lodges, fitted up with small lodge poles, and with all the furniture of a real lodge. They are playing at keeping house. By and by they will move their camp. Catching some of the old, steady dogs, and harnessing them to the travois, they will pack up their camp, set out on the march, and then going a short distance, put up the lodges again, build their fires and go to cooking, pounding berries, dressing hides, and doing all the things that occupy their mothers in the daily life of the camp.

On the outskirts of the camp, young people are engaged in different games and contests of skill. Young girls and women, fifteen or twenty of them, are running hither and thither after a large ball of buckskin, stuffed with antelope or buffalo hair. This is driven along the ground before the players with their feet, each one trying to retain the ball as long as possible. This is a girl's game, but some of the young married women of the camp are taking part in it, as well as two or three half-grown lads, who have not yet reached the age for hunting or going to war, or at which they feel it necessary to appear dignified. All the players take the greatest interest in the game, which is really a great romp, and they shout, scream, laugh, run, and push each other about, like the children that they are.

Other young people are practising at throwing certain special toys made for this purpose. One of these is a small curved piece of bone four inches in length, formed of a section of a buffalo's rib. One end is sharpened and tipped with horn, and in either margin of the rib near the other end, holes are drilled diagonally, in which the quills of stout feathers are inserted, so that the toy will fly evenly. The contestants cast these implements, by an underhand throw, horizontally over a flat surface, so that the bone shall strike on its convex side and ricochet along it. These toys are used chiefly over the ice in winter, and an expert thrower can send one a surprisingly long way. Other boys and girls throw long slender springy sticks, tipped with buffalo horn. These are thrown forward by one end, turning over and over in the air, and when the tip strikes the ground the stick bounds up, turns over several times, again strikes on the point and bounds into the air, thus advancing by leaps for a long distance.

No game played by men and boys is so popular as the stick or ring game. Little children begin to play it as soon as they can run easily, well-grown boys practice it constantly, and young men spend much of their time in camp racing over the course, winning and losing horses, arms, and clothing at the game. The stick game varies in some of its details with different tribes, but its essential features are everywhere the same. It is played with a ring or wheel of rawhide, usually wrapped or cross barred with rawhide strings to give it stiffness, and variously adorned with beads and little tags, each of which has some special meaning. Each player is armed with a straight, slender, pointed stick, five feet long, which is thrown at the ring as it is rolled along the ground, the object being to send the stick through the ring. The sticks are some times simple, or in tribes where the game has reached a high degree of development and become more complex, cross bars, hooks, and other projections are lashed to them. When the ring is rolled along the ground the players run after it and dart their sticks at it. The relation of the ring to some part of the stick determines the number of points won by the thrower.

In every camp where a long stay is made the young men, before many days have passed, clear away the grass, stones, and inequalities from a piece of level ground, making a smooth course over which the ring is to be rolled, and at this course, the men of the camp, young and old, gather daily to play and to look at the game and gamble on it. Ranged along the course stand the spectators, of both sexes, wrapped in their robes. Some are merely onlookers, too old or too lazy to take part in the game. Others await their turn. A few women, interested in the success of lover or newly married husband, stand among the men and eagerly watch the play. A very large proportion of the men in the camp are now, or have been, players of the game, and the course is the gathering place during the day for all the idle men in the camp. It is also the great betting ground, for not only do the players contest for a stake, but the spectators lay wagers on their favourites, losing and winning large amounts of property on a single game.

These games afford superb exhibitions of speed and skill. Stripped to breech-clout and moccasins, the two contestants, holding their sticks in their hands, bend forward, straining like greyhounds in the slips, eager to start on the course. Their naked bodies, superbly developed, are lithe and sinewy rather than muscular, but wonderfully tough and enduring, for they are kept at the very highest pitch of physical training by their simple wholesome food and by the constant exercise that they are taking—the labour of hunting, the long foot journeys to war, and such sports as they are now indulging in. Brown skins reflect the light, black hair blows out in the breeze, dark eyes roll as they watch each other, and long fingers nervously clasp and unclasp, fitting themselves to the finger holds on the sticks which they grasp. One of the pair of players holds his stick in his left hand, prepared to roll the ring with his right. When both are ready and all the bets have been made, he who holds the ring gives it a strong pitch forward and both dash after it, as it rolls along the course. Racing along on flying moccasins they soon overtake it, and as its speed slackens, they dart their stick at it by a curious underhand throw, endeavouring to transfix it. This they seldom succeed in doing, but usually one or both sticks touch the ring and knock it down, and points are counted by the distance of the ring from the different parts of the stick.

It is unusual for a player to send his stick through the ring, but if this is accomplished he has won the game. Much more often a number of courses have to be run before the issue is decided, for, as the points obtained by each player are always deducted from the score of his opponent, one of the players is always nothing. The contestants take turns in rolling the ring, so that each alternately suffers a slight delay in starting and the inconvenience of having to change his stick from one hand to the other.

In its highest development the game is complicated and affords much opportunity for dispute and wrangling. When the players cannot decide the questions involved to the satisfaction of both, they call one of the spectators to act as umpire and give a decision, which is always accepted without demur as final. Among the men no sport of the camp attracts so much attention and interest as the stick game, yet the women do not care especially for it, for they have amusements of their own.

As the sun gets low in the west many of the women put aside their daily tasks and devote a little time to recreation—gossip and gambling. Gathered in groups in the shade of the lodges, with babies on their backs or beside them on the ground, they laugh and chatter, giving each other the news of their families and of the camp in a manner quite worthy of a civilized drawing room. Many of them play the seed game, the two parties sitting in line facing each other, each woman having by her side the little pile of property she intends to wager—some bits of red cloth, a few strings of beads, some tobacco, and other things that people use. These are not put up as stakes, but each player's bet is represented by a stick put up against a similar stick wagered by her opponent. The game is not unlike throwing dice. Five plum stones, blackened and then variously marked on one side, are placed on a flat wicker basket about the size and shape of a tea plate, and by a quick jerk are thrown into the air and then caught in the basket as they come down. The marks on the upper surface of the stones so caught indicate the value of the throw, and the points gained or lost by the line of women on the side of the manipulator of the basket. Much mirth accompanies this game, and the talking and laughter are incessant. The winners chaff their opponents, and these reply to their jeers with quick jest and repartee.

In the social dances, which are usually given at

Pawnee Woman and Child

night, women as well as men take part. The dances
are held in a large lodge, and all the dancers and
many onlookers gather there soon after the evening
meal is eaten, and long before the dance begins.
Men and women alike have prepared themselves for
the festivities. The hair is neatly combed, newly
braided, and shining; fine clothing is worn with many
ornaments, and the faces gleam with fresh red paint.
The women sit together on one side of the lodge and
the men on the other. Long before the dancers step
on to the floor the singers—chosen for their skill—
start the air, which is usually in a minor key, and
keep time to the song by pounding on a drum or on a
parfleche which lies on the ground. To an unaccustomed ear many of the dance songs sound monotonous enough, yet often there is a great deal of
melody in them. Frequently a single dancer, man or
woman, will rise and dance for a long time alone,
stamping about with knees half bent; after a while
another joins in and then another, until half a dozen
may be dancing at the same time. As these retire
and sit down to rest, others take their place. Often a
woman gets up and dances for a time alone, and then
dancing before a particular man, chooses him for a
partner, and the two dance opposite one another with
deliberate steps for some time and then sit down, or
the woman may throw her robe over her partner's
head and kiss him, and then sit down, leaving him to
dance for a time alone. This is an expression of lik-
ing for the man and a high compliment to him. In
other dances the woman gives to the partner she has
selected some trifling present, and he is expected to
make one to her in return. Such dances are partici-
pated in for the most part by young people. The

dancers keep excellent time, and, while very much in earnest about the whole performance, seem greatly to enjoy themselves.

Many of the dances are performed in ordinary costume, except that both men and women throw off their robes or blankets to give them greater freedom and coolness, for dancing is hot work, and a lodge crowded with people is not the coolest place in the world. At special times, however, the men dance without any clothing except breech-clouts and moccasins and spend a great deal of time painting their bodies for the occasion. White clay is a favourite colour for legs and arms, and sometimes for the body; red is the colour most used for the face, and occasionally green and yellow.

At times there takes place a dance, which is almost wholly commercial. In the old days, when the tribes manufactured their own clothing, arms, utensils, and ornaments, it happened usually that each one was celebrated for some special article which it was known to make better than other tribes. It might be that one tribe made handsomer war bonnets, better war shirts, or louder rattles than its neighbours, and occasionally a few men would take a number of these desirable and high-priced articles and visit some neighbouring tribe to barter their goods for horses or other property. Hospitably received, they live in the lodges of principal men, and before long give a dance—usually one of those peculiar to their own tribe—in which perhaps some of the garments or ornaments which they have to sell are worn and so displayed, or if this is not done, the dance is at least an advertisement of their presence and its purpose.

Gambling is a universal amusement among Indians, and they bet on all games of skill and chance. The Indians of the Southwest have long been familiar with playing cards, and with these play some Spanish games, but, even at the present day, they prefer to lay wagers on their own games. They delight in horse-racing and foot-racing, and bet heavily on these as well as on the stick game; but perhaps no gambling game is so widespread and so popular as that known as "hands." It consists in guessing in which of the two hands is held a small marked object, right or wrong guessing being rewarded or penalized by the gain or loss of points. The players sit in lines facing each other, each man betting with the one opposite him. The object held, which is often a small polished bone, is intrusted to the best player on one side, who sits opposite to the best player on the other. The wagers are laid—after more or less discussion and bargaining as to the relative values of things as unlike as an otter-skin quiver on one side and two plugs of tobacco, a yard of cloth, and seven cartridges on the other—and the game begins with a low song, which soon increases in volume and intensity. As the singers become more excited, the man who holds the bone moves his hands in time to the song, brings them together, seems to change the bone rapidly from hand to hand, holds their palms together, puts them behind his back or under his robe, swaying his body back and forth, and doing all he can to mystify the player who is about to try to choose the bone. The other for a time keeps his eyes steadily fixed on the hands of his opponent, and, gradually as the song grows faster, bends forward, raises his right hand with extended forefinger above his head, and holds it there, and at last, when he is ready, with a swift motion brings it down to a horizontal, pointing at one of the hands which is instantly opened. If it contains the bone, the side which was guessing has won, and each man receives a stick from the opposite player. The bone is then passed across to the opposite side, the song is renewed, and the others guess. The game offers opportunities for cheating, but this seldom takes place. I have known of only one case of the kind, and in that instance the detected gamblers were forced by peaceful means to return all the property they had won. This was during the Crook campaign of 1876–'77, when the Cheyenne and Pawnee scouts who accompanied the command gambled against each other. At first the luck of the game varied in the usual way, but at last it turned to the side of the Cheyennes, who were occasionally able to guess which hand held the bone when the Pawnees had it, while the Pawnees never succeeded in guessing right when the Cheyennes had it.

This occurred so constantly that suspicion was excited and a close watch was kept on the Cheyenne player. When it was believed that he had hidden the bone in his robe, where he could drop his hand on it in a moment, two Pawnees sprang forward, and seizing his two hands held them up in the air closed, in the sight of all the players. They were opened and both were empty. A long wrangle followed in which the Cheyennes disavowed the act of their fellow, and at length agreed to restore, and did restore, all the horses that they had thus unfairly won.

Like most games of chance at which men win or lose property, this one has a strong fascination for the Indians, and men spend their nights at play and win and lose heavily.

On special occasions, when visits are being paid by members of another tribe, horse and foot racing take place. Each party bring out some swift pony or man, and bet on the champion all they have. If the visitors lose they will very likely receive many presents from their hosts, so that they may not be obliged to go home poor, but if they win, they may very likely carry with them nearly all the property of the camp, for the intense tribal pride of the Indian—his patriotism—leads him to believe that the men, women, children, and ponies of his own tribe can do things better than any others, and he will show his faith in his own by wagering his last pony and his last blanket on its performance.

Such are some of the principal pastimes of the people during the hours of a fair summer day. There are winter sports in which the children engage, sliding down hill on sleds made of buffalo ribs, spinning tops on the ice, and playing half naked in the snow. The tiny children sometimes find an old buffalo bull wallowing through the deep snow and delight in running up close to it and shooting at it their headless arrows. In winter the men no longer play at sticks; the women do their gambling in the lodge. But if food is abundant the feasting and the dancing and the visiting go on in all weathers.

CHAPTER III.

A MARRIAGE.

In the circle of the lodges stood one that was large and painted on all its sides with the story of its owner's deeds. From two of the lodge poles buffalo tails swung in the wind, and on a tripod near at hand hung the bundles which proclaimed the owner of the lodge to be a medicine man and a great warrior. This was the home of Three Suns, the chief of a gens of the people. He was a great chief, brave, wise, and generous. In the councils of the tribe be thought and spoke for the good of the people, not for himself; for many years he had been a leader of war parties and all his journeys to war had been lucky, for he had struck many of his enemies and had taken many horses. Most of these he gave away to his friends and relations or to those who were poor or to comfort those who had lost friends or relations in war.

Not far from the lodge of Three Suns, in the circle of the camp, stood the home of Buffalo Ribs, himself a chief, a brave warrior, successful in his expeditions against his enemies, rich from the spoils of war, a man of kindly heart and generous disposition, well thought of by all the tribe. Now Buffalo Ribs had a son, a young man of marriageable age, who as a servant had been off on two or three war parties, and had done well. He had taken some horses and was a good

30

hunter. This young man, whose name was White Antelope, had seen the oldest daughter of Three Suns, and because she was pleasant to look at he liked her, and he wanted her for his wife. He had spoken to her too; in the beginning only looking at her and smiling, and afterward waiting for her outside her father's lodge and talking to her—at first only a little, for she was afraid and would not wait to listen, but afterward, as she got used to him, he had talked to her longer, so that now the two knew each other well.

When White Antelope had made up his mind that he wanted this girl for his wife, and when he found that she liked him, he spoke to his father about the matter, telling what What in his mind; and Buffalo Ribs considering it, and remembering that Three Suns' family was good, and that he was a chief, loved by his people, and rich, and that his wives were good women and kept the lodge well supplied with dressed skins and good clothing, and that the girl was modest, quiet, sensible, and always busy, thought that she would make a good wife for his boy. So, when he had thought of all these things, he sent word to his brothers and nearest kinsfolk, asking them to come to his lodge and eat with him, for he had something to say to them. He told his wife to cook food, and she took from the parfleches dried corn and dried berries and dried meat and backfat, and boiled the food, and before sunset all was ready.

When the invited relations had come and all had eaten, and the pipe had been lighted and was passing from hand to hand around the circle, Buffalo Ribs spoke to his relations and told them what was in his mind and asked their opinion about this marriage, whether it ought to take place or not. Then they began to speak, one at a time, the oldest first, and some said one thing and some another, but all spoke good words about Three Suns and his girl, and all thought that it would be good if the young man could have her for his wife. When all had spoken, Buffalo Ribs himself stood up and spoke, and said that he thought as they all did, and that it was his purpose to ask Three Suns for the girl to be the wife of White Antelope. So the matter was concluded.

The next day, when the sun was high, the mother of White Antelope went to the lodge of Three Suns and spoke to his first wife, telling her how it was, and that Buffalo Ribs wanted her daughter for his son's wife; and Three Suns' woman listened, but said nothing. When Three Suns came again to his camp from his hunting, the women took the meat from the horses and turned them loose. Then afterward, when he had eaten and was smoking, as he sat there resting, the woman told him what Buffalo Ribs' wife had said. For a long time the chief sat there and smoked, saying nothing, for he was thinking; but at length he knocked the ashes from his pipe and spoke to the woman, saying: "Make ready something to eat, and I will send word to my close relations and ask them to come and eat with me, a little time before the sun disappears behind the mountains." His wife answered: "It shall be as you have said." She called the other women, and they prepared a kettleful of dried meat and sarvis berries and hung it over the fire, and from the parfleches took dried backfat and tongues, and made ready for a feast. Three Suns called to a young man who lay asleep in the shade of a lodge near by, and said to him: "Go now to the lodges of Skunk Head, Took Two Guns, Buffalo Horse,

He Struck Two, and Wolf Moccasin, and tell them that I ask them to come and smoke with me a little while before the sun goes to rest behind the mountains." And the young man arose and went away.

When the time came, and the sun was getting low, these invited men came to Three Suns' lodge and entered, and as they came in the host spoke to each one, bidding him welcome and showing him where to sit. To his oldest relations he gave the seats furthest from the door, while the younger ones sat further from himself. When all had come, the women set food before them, and, while they were eating, Three Suns was cutting tobacco and fixing the pipe for smoking. At length the dishes were cleared, the women took them away, and the pipe, having been loaded, was passed by Three Suns to the young man on his right, who lighted it and handed it back. Then Three Suns made a prayer and smoked to the sky, to the earth, and to the four points of the compass, and handed the pipe to the old man on his left hand. He smoked and made a prayer, and passed it to the next, who did the same, and he to the next, and so it went around, each man making a prayer. When he had smoked, Three Suns spoke, and told his relations of the message sent him by Buffalo Ribs, and asked them what they thought about the matter, and whether the marriage that had been proposed ought to take place. For a little while no one spoke, and then the oldest of the relations, Skunk Head, the uncle of Three Suns, said: "My opinion is that the girl should be given to that young man. We all know Buffalo Ribs, a brave man, lucky in war, careful of his people, generous and rich. He has many horses, and is often away upon the warpath getting more, but when has he lost one of his young men? He has good women, not foolish ones, and they are always busy. The young man, his son, has done well. Four times he has been to war, and all his journeys have been fortunate. He will be like his father, and though now he is only a servant, yet, if he survives, the time will come when he will be a brave, and it may be a chief. My son's* daughter is a good woman, and she will make a good wife, caring well for her husband's comfort, and bringing up good children. Therefore let these young people sit beside each other and be man and wife." When he had finished, most of those sitting there said it was good. Then one or two others spoke, saying the same things that Skunk Head had said. Then Three Suns said: "For myself, I think with all of you, that it is well that my daughter should be given to this young man. It shall be done as you have said." Some more talk followed, as is natural among relations, and then one by one the men left the lodge.

While these older people were talking thus, the young people were talking too. From Three Suns' lodge a well-worn trail led through the sage brush toward the stream and entered the fringe of the willows and underbrush that grew along its banks, and down this trail, with quick light steps and a contented smile upon her face, Three Suns' daughter was passing. She was neatly—even handsomely—dressed, her buckskin moccasins ornamented with bright-coloured quills, and her leggings and gown beaded and fringed, while many elk tushes were sewed to its sleeves and shoulders and made a light rattling sound as she

---

*The Indian calls his nephews sons and his nieces daughters.

walked. Her hair was newly braided and shining, and her cheeks, forehead, and the parting of her hair were bright with fresh paint. About her throat was a many-coloured collar of small beads, embroidered with sinew thread on a strip of soft-dressed buckskin in a curious pattern, while from her leggings hung two or three little brass bells which tinkled softly as she walked, and with the faintly rattling elk teeth made a little chime to her movements.

The fringe of bushes bordering the stream was only a few yards wide, but as the girl approached it she looked ahead earnestly, as if expecting to see something. Just within the bushes, in a little opening at the side of the trail, stood a tall figure shrouded from head to ankles in a dressed cow skin sheet, which concealed the whole person. A corner of the sheet was drawn over the head, and the eyes looked out through a narrow slit. Evidently the girl knew who it was, for when she saw the figure she smiled a little to herself, held down her head, and turned her face away, but continued her brisk walk along the trail. Just as she had come opposite the figure and was about to pass by, it took a swift step forward, the sheet opened and closed again about the girl, who with a faint exclamation dropped her bucket and stood, held close in her lover's arms.

Their conference was a long one, but at length the girl wrenched herself free, picked up her bucket, ran to the water's edge, and filled it, and without a word glided away along the trail toward the camp.

That night a message was sent to Buffalo Ribs, telling him that the proposal of marriage was acceptable to Three Suns, and at once the two families began to prepare for the events. There was a natural

4

desire on the part of each to give the two young people a good start in life; but besides this, as both families were well to do and of high social standing in the
tribe, the members of each were ambitious that their
marriage gifts should exceed in value those of the
other family. This rivalry promised a generous out-
fitting for the pair. So it was that all the relations
on either hand began to consider what they should give.

First of all, the wives of Three Suns began to make
ready the special property, which in a marriage between wealthy people the girl always brings with
her. From her store of newly dressed cow skins,
white and smooth, the principal wife of Three Suns
chose sixteen large ones, and after going over them
carefully, and sewing up with sinew the arrow and bullet holes, she spread out these skins and cut them so
as to form the lodge. Then taking the bundles of
sinew thread made from the ligaments which lie along
the loin of the buffalo, Three Suns' wives and older
daughters began the work of sewing together the
lodge. Many hands make light work, and in two or
three days the task was accomplished. Next were
selected eighteen new lodge poles, slender yet strong,
smoothly shaved down with a knife, so that no knots,
splinters, or rough bark remained on them, by which
the lodge covering might be worn or torn, and pointed
at their butts so that they should not slip on the
smooth hard ground. The two longer poles, which
support the ears, or wings on either side the smoke-
hole, were pointed at their upper ends as well, so that
the loops at the points of the wings should fit over
them and should not slip off when blown by the wind.
Besides this lodge, there was supplied a lining for it,
back rests, parfleches to pack with and to contain

food, utensils with which to prepare, cook, and serve it, buckets and cups for water—in fact, all the furniture of a home. Many of these articles had already been made by the women of the family, many others were sent to the lodge as presents by the girl's relations.

Besides the clothing which the girl already possessed, there were provided new gowns, leggings, and moccasins, all of them embroidered with beads and bright quills, and ornamented with fringe and with strips of fur or red or blue cloth. The gowns were made of buck or elk skin carefully tanned, smooth and flexible, smoked so as not to harden when they become wet, and then carefully whitened with white clay. The leggings were of buckskin. The girl's summer sheet was the well-tanned skin of a buffalo heifer, or of an elk, on which the dew claws had been left. After it had been tanned and smoked, its outer surface —that from which the hair had been removed—was thoroughly rubbed with white clay, after which the skin was beaten to remove the superfluous earth. This was repeated from time to time as the sheet became soiled, and so it was always white and new looking.

To his oldest daughter, Three Suns had already given two riding horses and a pack horse, and she already had her own riding saddle—high peaked in front and behind, and fringed with buckskin, with an embroidered saddlecloth—as well as a pack saddle. Very likely another saddlecloth will be given her, made from a part of a buffalo robe, tanned very soft, the upper surface—the flesh side of the robe—embroidered with beads and bordered with red or blue cloth which is also beaded. Perhaps one of her brothers, or her mother, may have made for her riding horse a headstall of rawhide, which she has wound with beads and adorned with two or three brass bells. Among the various household utensils especially required by a girl about to be married are knives for butchering, mauls, large and small, scrapers and fleshers for tanning hides, pots and kettles for cooking, vessels to hold water and cups to drink from, dishes to eat from, spoons, and ladles. All these various articles the girl will receive, in much the same way as a young woman of our day and civilization receives her trousseau and her wedding gifts. Her mother and father supply the lodge, the robes, the clothing, and besides all this a dowry of horses. The father also often presents to his son-in-law his own weapons of war and his war clothing. Such a gift means more than the mere value of the articles, though usually this is not small, and, besides, they are endeared to their owner by many associations. It is an evidence of the high esteem in which he holds the young man, and is an unspoken assurance that the donor believes his son-in-law will use these things with as much credit to himself as their former owner. It is the highest compliment that a man can pay to his son-in-law.

While all the preparations for the marriage were going on Three Suns' daughter had to face a trial. When it had been decided that she should become the wife of White Antelope, she had to do something very hard—a thing which would tell the people of the camp that the marriage was to take place.

The next morning after the matter had been de-termined, Three Suns' daughter selected some food, the best that there was in the lodge, cooked it, and when it was ready to be eaten, she put it in a bowl, covered it with a dish, and then clad in her best clothes and followed by her younger sister, she left her father's lodge and walked toward that occupied by Buffalo Ribs. All the people whom she passed, sitting or standing about the camp, looked curiously at her as she went by them, and some of the young people giggled and whispered together. The girl felt very much ashamed, but she walked along with her eyes cast down, her sister following modestly behind her, and soon reached the lodge to which she was going and entered it. Turning to the left she sat down for a moment on the woman's side, so as to see who was there, and she was glad when she found that the only people within were White Antelope, who was at work smoothing arrowshafts between two stones, and Buffalo Ribs' first wife and daughter, who were sewing moccasins. When the girl saw that these were the only people in the lodge, she rose, and going to where White Antelope sat, she offered the dish to him. He took it and ate, and the girl returned to her place and sat down. After the boy had eaten, he put down the dish on the ground before him, and went on with his work, and the girl again rising, took the dish and offered it to his mother, who also ate a little, and then put it down. A few moments after this the daughters of Three Suns left the lodge and walked back toward their father's. As she was returning the girl still held her eyes down and looked neither to the right nor to the left, but it seemed to her that the people did not stare so much, and that the boys and girls did not titter and talk so much about her.

During the whole time between the acceptance of the proposal and the marriage the girl thus brought food each day to White Antelope, serving him as a wife should serve her husband, and thus telling all the people that they were to be man and wife.

During the days of preparation for the marriage, which usually are not many, the relations of Three Suns were bringing their presents to the lodge. The men brought men's things and the women things used by women, and by the time the day had come there might be two or three horseloads of gifts. When all was ready, the mother and daughter packed all these things on some of the horses with the new lodge and lodge poles, and moving off to near where Buffalo Ribs' gens was camped, the horses were unpacked, the lodge was put up, the furniture was moved into it, a fire was kindled, and the horses belonging to the girl and those presented by the relations were tied outside the lodge. Then the mother went back to her home. As soon as she had gone, White Antelope, perhaps accompanied by one of his young brothers, drove up his horses and tied them near the lodge and entered. Thus the marriage was accomplished.

Before this, the boy or his father and his relations had got together the horses which were to be sent to Three Suns. They all wished to be considered generous, and they made it a point to send to the chief presents of greater value than those which the girl had received from her family. These presents were, many of them, distributed among those relations who had made gifts to the girl. Soon after the marriage, feasts were given by the two families in honour of the newly married pair, and on such occasions, those of the girl's relations who had received gifts sent to Three Suns by Buffalo Ribs or his family, made presents of like value to the young people. So all the presents given by both families came back at last to the newly married pair.

It is of course understood that the marriage customs of different tribes vary widely, and that, even within the same tribe, no two marriages take place in precisely the same way. Among the poor and the unimportant there is much less ceremony than among those who are of good family and well to do.

As an example of the ways of a particular tribe—the Pawnees—the following account* is given:

In the olden time, before they had horses, when their dogs, their simple arms, and their clothing constituted all their possessions, the Pawnees married for love. The affection which existed between two young people was then the only motive which brought about a union, and this affection was seldom interfered with unless there was a very great difference between the social standing of the family of the boy and of the girl, for it must be understood that even in primitive times rank existed in a Pawnee camp, just as it does to-day in civilized society.

After the Pawnees obtained horses and began to accumulate property—as the people acquired wealth, and their circumstances became easier—the practice arose of giving presents to the immediate relatives of the girl whose hand was sought in marriage. These presents were given in order to conciliate those relations who controlled the girl. Originating merely in this desire to gain the good will of her family, the custom gradually became more and more firmly established until it had come to be a matter of course to give presents, and finally a matter of necessity if the young man hoped to gain the consent of the girl's family to his proposal of marriage. The presents at

*Marriage among the Pawnees. American Anthropologist, July, 1891.

first were probably small in value and number, but in a case where there was more than one suitor for the girl there would naturally be a rivalry on the part of the families of the young men, and each would strive to help the cause of its own member by presenting gifts more valuable than those offered by the other. Young men of standing and position would put forth every effort to make the families of the women they loved presents as handsome as had their fellows who had married, and all this would have its influence on families who counted marriageable girls among their number. Parents and relatives, at first receiving these as evidences of friendship and good will, would at length come to regard them as their due, and would ultimately insist on receiving them as a condition of giving their consent to the marriage proposal, thinking themselves injured and even defrauded if they were not forthcoming; so little by little the matter of obtaining a wife grew to be regarded, not only by the suitor and the girl's father, but by the tribe at large, as an actual purchase of the woman.

Among the Pawnees, however, these presents were not always, nor, I believe, even usually, regarded as a price paid for the girl. They did not speak of them otherwise than as presents made to her family. Often the gifts were not decided on until after the marriage had taken place. A father would give his daughter to a young man of a good family or one who was well to do without making any stipulations as to what the presents should be, and a Pawnee young man might say, "I am going to marry such a girl. It is left to me what I shall do afterward." (Tŭt ki′tta wi i′ri la tīts ka, lŭ′t kŭt.)

A young man did not expect to marry until he had

come to be an expert hunter, and so was able to support a wife. This gave him standing with the parents, who would naturally be more willing to give their daughter to a good provider. Nor did he usually think about taking a wife until he had been on the warpath and either brought back some horses or had struck an enemy. This would give him favour in the eyes of the young women.

When a young man had determined that he wishes to marry he perhaps courted the girl in the usual way, or, if he had no fondness for any particular young woman, he spoke to his parents and announced to them his wish to take a wife.

In case the boy had merely decided that he wished to marry and had not himself made a choice, his relations talked the matter over and selected a girl. This having been done, some old man was called in, and asked to conduct the negotiations between the two families. Usually, if it was convenient, the man selected for this purpose—at least among the Skidi— was a priest, one greased with the sacred fat of the buffalo. Such a man's influence with the family he was about to visit would be stronger than that of a common man, and he would be more likely to receive a favourable answer.

On a chosen day this old man and the suitor would prepare themselves for a visit to the lodge of the girl's father. The old man would paint his face with red earth, while the boy would also paint himself, put beads about his neck, and don his best attire, his finest leggings and moccasins worked with quills or beads. Both then put on their robes, hair side out, and late in the afternoon, about four or five o'clock, they started toward the lodge where the girl lived, the old man leading the way, the young one following at his heels.

Of course, when the people of the camp saw an old man followed by a young one, both wearing their robes hair side out, walking through the village, they knew that a proposal of marriage was going to be made, and usually a pretty shrewd guess could be hazarded as to the lodge they were going to. If the father of any girl suspected that his lodge was to be visited, he would hurry home, to be there to receive the ambassador and aspirant.

When the men reached the lodge they entered and squatted by the fire just to the right of the door, ready to take their departure if they were not made welcome. If the father was at home he would speak to the old man, who would explain to him the object of the visit. Then the visitors would go out of the lodge and return to that of the boy's family. It might sometimes happen that there was more than one marriageable girl in the lodge, and then, in the absence of the father, the oldest person in the lodge would inquire of the old man which girl it was whose hand was sought, and after learning would ask the visitors to go home and return later.

The same evening they would come back to the lodge and find many or most of the girl's relations. Those who were unable to come have sent word that they agree to whatever the others may decide on. These relations have thoroughly discussed the young man, his social standing, his skill as a hunter, his prowess in war, and his general desirability as a member of the family, and have determined what answer shall be made to the offer of marriage. When the two men enter the lodge the second time, if they see a robe or blanket spread for them to sit on, they know that they are welcome and that the answer will be favourable. If no seat is provided they go away at once; their proposal is declined.

After speeches have been made by the girl's relations, one of them takes a pipe and lights it. He prays, blows a few puffs to the sky, to the earth, and to the four cardinal points, and then offers it to the old man, saying, as he does so, "I hope that you will take pity on us, for we are poor." This seems to be at once an expression of good feeling and a hope that the young people may get along well together—may have no trouble after they are married.

The old man smokes first, and then the relation offers the pipe to the suitor, who does the same, both saying, *La'wa i'ri.* When this has been done the two rise and retire, the old man taking the robe or blanket on which they have been sitting as his present from the girl's relations. On returning to the young man's lodge they report to his relations assembled there the result of their visit, and satisfaction is expressed at its favourable outcome. The presents for the girl's family are now contributed by the boy's relations. They consist of blankets, robes, guns, horses, and so on, and are usually taken on the same night to the lodge where the girl lives by one of the young man's relations—his mother, aunt, or sister. On being received they are distributed among the relations of the girl.

Early next morning the young man is invited for the first time over to the lodge where the girl lives. Before he arrives the girl has combed her hair, put on her best clothing, and is sitting on a robe in the most honourable seat, far back in the lodge. When the young man comes in, a cushion or pillow is placed by

the side of the girl, and her father or some of her relations tells him to sit down by her side. The girl
then rises, takes a dish containing food, which she
places before him, and they both eat. The girl is now
his wife, and he stays here and makes his home in her
father's lodge for a time, usually until he has some
children and feels that he can set up a lodge of his
own.

It was not infrequently the case, where a girl had
two or three suitors that her parents might wish her to
marry one, while she preferred another. Very severe
measures were often resorted to in order to force her
to marry the one chosen by the family, and unless she
could succeed in running away with the man of her
choice she usually had to yield to the family influence.

Younger sisters were the potential wives of the
husband of the oldest girl. If a married man died,
his wives became the wives of his oldest brother.

A word or two with regard to the position of the
wife in the household may not be out of place here.
The Indian woman, it is usually thought, is a mere
drudge and slave, but, so far as my observations ex-
tend, this notion is wholly an erroneous one. It is
true that the women were the labourers of the camp;
that they did all the hard work about which there was
no excitement. They cooked, brought wood and water, dried the meat, dressed the robes, made the clothing, collected the lodge poles, packed the horses, cultivated the ground, and generally performed all the
tasks which might be called menial, but they were not
mere servants. On the contrary, their position was
very respectable. They were consulted on many subjects, not only in connection with family affairs, but
in more important and general matters. Sometimes

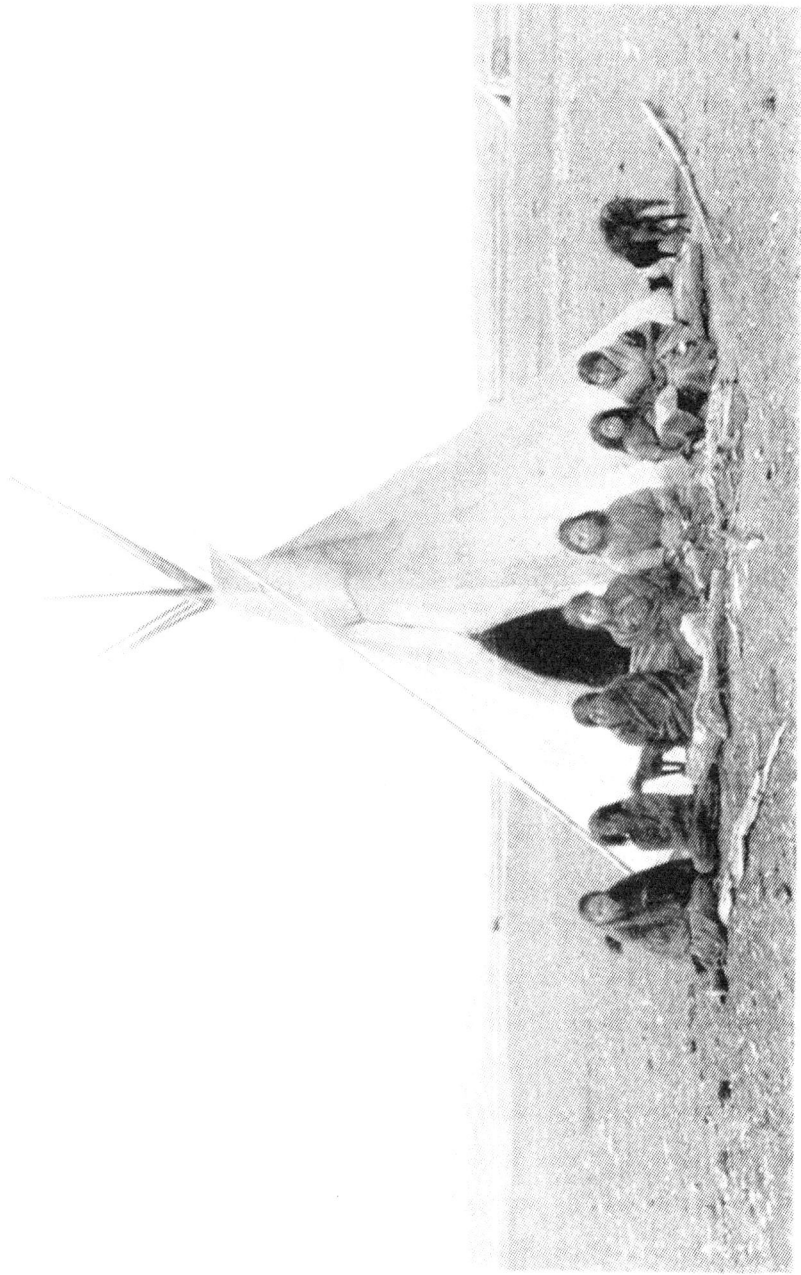

Piegan Women and Children

women were even admitted to the councils and spoke there, giving their advice. This privilege was very unusual, and was granted only to women who had performed some deed which was worthy of a man. This in practice meant that she had killed or counted *coup* on an enemy, or had been to war.

In ordinary family conversation women did not hesitate to interrupt and correct their husbands when the latter made statements with which they did not agree, and the men listened to them with respectful attention, though of course this depended on the standing of the woman, her intelligence, etc. While their lives were hard and full of toil, they yet found time to get together for gossip and for gambling, and on the whole managed to take a good deal of pleasure in life.

CHAPTER IV.

SUBSISTENCE.

THE life of the Indian was in some respects a hard one, for the question of food was an ever-present anxiety with him. We are told in books much about the Indian's improvidence, and it is frequently stated that however abundant food might be with him to-day, he took no thought for the needs of the morrow. Such statements are untrue, and show but superficial observation. The savage does not look so far ahead as does the civilized man, but still the lessons of experience are not wholly lost on him. He remembers past hardships, and endeavours to provide against their recurrence; and these people were rather remarkable for their foresight, and for the provision which they were accustomed to make for the future. The tribes which tilled the ground, dried the corn, beans, and squashes which they grew, and usually had enough of these to last them until the next crop was harvested; others which were not agriculturists gathered at the different seasons of the year, when they were ripe, great quantities of berries and roots of various kinds, which were dried and stored in sacks made of parfleche, or of woven grass or reeds, until such time as they should be needed. This surplus food was not always carried about with them, but was hidden in *caches,* which were visited from time to time as the food was required. The Indians of the plains who depended for subsistence largely on the buffalo, dried great stores of its flesh against times of need, and this dried meat—which would keep for an indefinite length of time—was used to make the nutritious pemmican.

Many of the mountain tribes made annual pilgrimages to the plains for buffalo meat—choosing especially the season at which the animals were fat and the skins in good condition for robes—and in this way secured a portion of their winter's supply of meat; but the mountain tribes depended largely on the flesh of mountain game—deer, elk, wild sheep, and goats—which they hunted persistently and with great success. The meat of these animals was dried.

Still further to the west the Indians, as summer drew on, began to gather along the streams up which the salmon run to spawn. By means of traps, gaffs, spears, and dip nets, they took each season enormous quantities of fish, which were sun or smoke dried and packed away in *caches*. These were rough wooden boxes made of "shakes"—rough planks or slabs wedged off from the trunk of the white cedar or arborvitæ. For protection against the ravages of wild animals or insects, these *caches* were usually placed high up in the branches of a tree. In this position they were, of course, visible to the passer-by, but were never disturbed, the property of others always being respected. Only in the case of people actually perishing of hunger would anything be taken from such a *cache,* and in cases of such extremity the disturber was welcome to what he needed.

Finally, when we reach the coast, we find a people who lived principally on the products of the sea, but who still were at home in the mountains. These were canoe people, and in their frail barks, burned and whittled out of the trunk of a great cedar tree, they made long journeys to the fishing banks for halibut, or to the rocks for fur seal and sea lion, or followed the sea otter or chased and killed the whale. Following up the inlets or the mouths of the rivers, they captured the salmon with the two-pronged spear, or, anchored in some narrow channel, swept the long fish rake through the shoals of herring, taking them by canoeloads. When the delicate oolachan, or candlefish, came to the beaches to spawn, they gathered them for their flesh and oil. In the spring and autumn, when the coat of the white goat was long and shaggy, they climbed the steep mountain sides to its home and killed it for its meat and for the fleece, which the women wove into warm and durable blankets. In summer, they watched at lakes and in little mountain parks to shoot deer, or coasted along the seashore and killed them when they came down to the beach to feed on the seaweed, or again in winter, when the snows had driven them thither from the thick timber, which is their usual haunt. Most of this work was done by the men. The women gathered berries and dried them for winter use, and collected dulse along the shore.

Further to the south there were different ways among the different tribes, depending on the various products of the territory inhabited. The Indians of Nevada and Utah captured great numbers of jack rabbits by surrounding them, and drove the locusts into pits. The coast Indians of southern California subsisted largely on shellfish. Some tribes made a bread of the dried sweet acorn of the California oak. In the central region pine nuts, and further south the bean of the mesquite, served the same purpose. The Pueblo tribes of New Mexico and Arizona cultivated the ground, raising corn by means of irrigation, which they had practised from time immemorial. The desert-inhabiting Navajo and Apache still eat the fruit of the cactus and roast mescal roots.

Although the larger animals were the most important source of food supply, it must not be supposed that the smaller ones were neglected. Wild cats, beavers, skunks, prairie dogs, ground squirrels, rats, and all birds were eaten when they could be had, not always from necessity, but because they were good for food. These were taken in traps and snares, and usually by the boys.

The Indian made the most of what his country produced, and in time of abundance strove to lay up provisions against the day of want. When the buffalo were plenty, he rioted in slaughter and feasted fat, and dried much meat and tongues and backfat. If the run of salmon was large, he caught all that he could, and his drying scaffolds far up the hillside shone red against the background of green; if the berry or the root crop was plentiful, the women worked hard to gather and dry them in great quantities. For a day might come when no buffalo could be found, when the salmon would not run up the river, and the root or berry crop would fail. Bitter experience had taught the Indian that he might at any time have to face starvation.

The Indian recognises that his whole life is a contest with Nature, that all her powers are opposed to him. He realizes his own feebleness, and sees that to procure subsistence he must overcome Nature and wrest a livelihood from her unwilling grasp. He can

5

only gain the victory and be successful in his under-
takings if he has the help of some stronger power,
some force which is higher than Nature—which rules
it—so, literally, "looking through Nature up to Nature's God," he appeals to his god for assistance, and
to win the Deity over to his side, and also to show
how much in earnest he is, he offers sacrifices of food,
tobacco, ornaments, a lock of his hair, or a bit of his
flesh. Since without food life is impossible, all important hunting expeditions were preceded by religious
ceremonies more or less elaborate, which had for their
object the propitiation of the Deity and the obtaining
his help. The Pawnees, before they started on the
hunt, devoted several days to religious observances—
fasting, praying, and dancing, under the direction of
the priests, asking for assistance in the hunt, for
plenty of buffalo, and, as always in their prayers, for
long life, health, and strength. With them also the
first deer or buffalo slain in the hunt was always sacrificed to the Deity. In the same way the Rees, Mandans, and Gros Ventres of the village prefaced their
hunts by religious ceremonies. Among some tribes
no general observance of this kind took place, but he
who acted the chief part in the work of trapping the
buffalo spent the night before he entered on his task
in prayer, and the priests—those whose petitions to
the Deity were supposed to be most efficacious—devoted much time to offering up prayers for the success of the drive.

The enormous multitudes of buffalo that fed on the
plains and in the mountains of the West made it usually an easy matter in modern times for the tribes to
supply themselves with food, and yet the buffalo were
not sure to be always at hand. They were as nomadic

as the Indians, and sometimes moved away from any given region and did not reappear for months, so that the food stored up by the people became entirely exhausted. They were then obliged to turn their attention to the smaller game, antelope, deer, and elk, which they could kill about their camps, but these animals could never be relied on for support. For this reason, it was the practice among many of the buffalo-eating tribes to send runners out to make long journeys to find the buffalo, and, by watching them, to learn in what direction they were tending, and then to report as quickly as possible to the camp.

When it is remembered how abundant and how unsuspicious of danger the buffalo were in the early days in the West, it might be imagined that the vigorous and active Indian—a footman who was always on the march, and nearly as swift and enduring as the buffalo—would, under ordinary conditions, have been able always to keep himself supplied with food, even though he carried only a bow and arrows as his weapon. But such a conclusion would be erroneous.

It is difficult for us who dwell among the civilized surroundings of this age to realize how severe was the struggle for existence of primitive man in America; what the condition of the Indian was in the days before the white man had come, bringing with him firearms which kill at a distance and horses which can overtake the buffalo. To comprehend this, we must stop and think, trying to move ourselves some centuries back to the time of the stone age, when the people, wholly without knowledge of metal, slew with weapons made of flint the wild beasts on which they subsisted, and moved from place to place on foot, car-

rying their simple possessions on their backs or on
the dog travois.

In those days the securing of daily food must have
been a difficult matter for many tribes, and the laying
up of any provision for the future doubly hard. The
great beasts, so easily slaughtered by the rifle, or even
by the iron-headed arrow shot into them at a close
range by a mounted man, must have been well-nigh
invulnerable to the stone-headed arrow. The tough
thick hide, covered with a close mat of fur, presents
resistance to the keen edge of a modern knife, and
could have been pierced only by the best arrows of
that day, shot at very short range; and if the careful
hunter crept close enough to the buffalo, and his arm
was strong enough to drive the blunt-headed shaft
deep into the body, the great beast, irritated by the
prick of the puny dart, instead of running away, might
turn to fight the one who had injured it. Often, no
doubt, the man kept out of sight and shot arrow after
arrow into it, for there was no sound to alarm it, and
it could not tell whence the hurt came; but let the
animal learn the cause of this pain, and the man was
in great danger.; for a wounded buffalo was a terrible
antagonist, swift of foot, resistless in power, only to
be avoided by the exercise of that cunning which
has ever given man the mastery over the brute. In
that age of stone the contest between wild man and
wild beast was not an unequal one. The beast was
the stronger, the quicker, the better armed of the two.
Man's advantage lay altogether in his intelligence.

Traces of the fear in which these great brutes were
held may still be discovered in the traditional stories
of certain tribes, which set forth how in those days,
before men were provided with arms, the buffalo used

to chase, kill, and eat the people. Such tales, still given with considerable detail among the Blackfeet, the Arikaras, and other tribes, show very clearly how greatly the buffalo were dreaded in ancient times, and such fear could hardly have arisen save as the result of actual experience of their power to inflict injury and death. If the buffalo had always been found to be the stupid but timorous animal that he was in the later days of the great herds, stories such as these could not have gained currency or persisted, and it seems clear that all of these traditional stories have some basis of fact and are in some measure founded on experience. Lapse of time, the changes which would inevitably result from the transmission of a tale through succeeding generations of narrators, and an imperfect comprehension of the relations of things may, in a measure, have twisted and distorted the fact or the experience; but if it is possible to trace the tale far enough, the fact and the circumstance will always be found.

Long before the time of the bow and arrows there must have been a day when for these men—the ancestors of the Indians whom we know—the capture of such a great animal as the buffalo was an impossibility, a thing altogether beyond their power to compass, and not to be contemplated: a time when the food of the people consisted of the fruits of the earth and the small animals; those which were so numerous, so timid, and so lacking in craft or wariness, that even feeble man, armed only with his club—the first weapon—could circumvent and kill them. In some of the tribes there still persist traditions of those earliest times, when arms—the bow and arrow, the shield and lance—were unknown, and many of the

practices of those ancient times have endured even to
the present day. The Blackfeet tell of a time when
they had no arms and lived on roots and berries, and
detail early methods of capturing animals; and the
Cheyenne traditions go back to the days when they
subsisted altogether on rabbits, the skins of which
furnished also their clothing. Some of the tribes of
the central plateau in our own day secured their food
of rabbits and grasshoppers by simple methods which
are very old; and in the ways in which the women of
all tribes gather berries and roots, and in which boys
with long slender whips kill birds, we see the survival
of practices which have a great antiquity. The invention of the bow and arrow—the traditional history
of which is given by many tribes—marked a tremendous step in advance of these early methods, and yet
even this invention still left the Indian but meagrely
equipped for the struggle with the great beasts which
were furnishing him with food at the time that he
was discovered by the white man. Old men still tell
of hearing their grandfathers speak of the complaints
made by their ancestors of the difficulty of obtaining
food in primitive times; of how often they were hungry, and how constantly they were moving about to
find regions where animals were more numerous and
more easily to be approached. Often such statements
come out incidentally in the course of conversation,
or are made to explain certain wanderings of which
tradition speaks.

Since his armament was so inefficient as to make
the capture of game at all times uncertain, and since
the effort to secure it was often attended with danger,
it must early have occurred to the Indian to devise
for capturing food in quantity some method which

should be more certain and more safe than the bow and arrow. The problem was long pondered over, and the first steps toward solving it, no doubt, took the direction of improving the traps and snares which they employed for the capture of the smaller animals, and the evolution of the pen with the extended wings, into which the buffalo or antelope were brought and captured whole herds at a time, was slow. On the other hand, in those early, as in more modern days, the Indian's whole study was the animals among which he lived. Constantly engaged in watching them and trying to learn how they would act under particular conditions, he knew their habits better than he knew anything else. Long before the traps, so successfully used, were devised he must have known of the existence in buffalo and antelope of that curiosity which made the trap feasible, and which to the animals proved so self-destructive.

Scattered along the flanks of the Rocky Mountains, and at many points of the great central plateau, may be seen to-day the remains of the ancient traps in which the Indians once took the buffalo. Most of the tribes gave up their use many years ago—soon after they obtained horses and learned to ride—and all the more perishable portions of wings and enclosures have long since crumbled to decay; but in various localities in Montana and Colorado the plains are still marked by the long lines of heaped-up stones which formed the arms of the chute that guided the doomed animals toward the cliff or the slaughter pen.

The common method* of taking buffalo, by those

---

*An account substantially like this was given by me in Scribner's Magazine for September, 1893, entitled The Last of the Buffalo.

tribes which inhabited the broken country close to the mountains, was to build a V-shaped chute, the arms of which extended far out on the prairie and came together at the top of a cliff, or a cut bank, over which the buffalo were expected to fall. If the cliff was high and vertical, the fall killed or crippled most of the animals, but if it was only a cut bank of moderate height, an enclosure was built at the foot of the bank below the angle of the V, from which the animals could not escape after they had made the plunge. We may imagine that originally they attempted always to drive the buffalo over high cliffs, where the fall would kill them, and that the enclosure was a later development from this.

The building of one of these traps involved a great deal of labour and took a long time, but after it had been completed, it was practically indestructible, and with annual repairs would last for generations. A spot was chosen beneath a convenient cut bank in a valley, usually near timber. With their rude tools they cut down the trees, and then dragged them near to the foot of a bank, and here the wall of the pen was raised, logs, rocks, poles, and brushwood being used to make a wall six or eight feet high, and so close that it could not be seen through. No special pains were taken to make it strong, for it was quite certain that the imprisoned buffalo would not dash themselves against it and try to push the wall down—although if at any point it was low, some very active animal might try to leap over it, or if there were large open spaces in the wall, one of them might attempt to burst through it; but there was no danger that they would surge against it in a mass, and so break it down and escape. While the pen was being built some of the women and boys were busy on the prairie above, bringing—often from a great distance on their backs or on the dog travois—stones to make the rock piles for the chute. These were heaped up in piles four or five feet high and six or eight in circumference, and were distant from each other from twenty to thirty feet. If the country was not stony, clusters of bushes were sometimes set up in the ground in place of the heaps of stones.

Modifications of this form of trap were used by the Cheyennes, who constructed their pen in a valley on a buffalo trail which was in use. It was sometimes built in a grove of trees, both for convenience in getting the logs and poles to form the walls, and because the standing trees served as supports for the wall, or, again, they built it under a cut bank, which thus constituted a part of the wall, and the wings stretched out on the level valley. Near the entrance to the pen, men lay hid to close it after the animals had gone in, using poles and brush, or poles alone, over which they hung robes. The northernmost of the three tribes of the Blackfoot confederation, and also the Plains Crees, both of whom lived at a distance from the mountains and in a country which was rolling rather than broken, made their pens on level ground not far from timber, where they secured the logs and brush for the walls. As elsewhere explained, the buffalo passed down the chute in the ordinary way, and at the angle of the V ran onto a fenced causeway, or bridge, which led them by a slight incline up to the level of a low point in the wall, from which they jumped down into the pen. When the last of the band had entered, men, hidden near by, quickly put poles across the low places in the wall and hung robes over them so as to make the wall appear continuous. Traps similar in most respects to these were used by some tribes for taking antelope in rather recent times; so lately that I have seen remains of the wooden wings and corral in northwestern Utah, in the country ranged over by Utes, Cheyennes, and Arapahoes. The Blackfeet also captured antelope in the same way, but instead of a pen at the angle of the V, they dug a large pit there, which they covered with a loose roof made of slender poles, twigs, and grass. When the antelope ran over the pit they broke through this roof, and falling into the pit were unable to get out again, and were easily secured by the men who were hidden near at hand.

It may naturally enough be asked how these wild animals were induced to enter these traps in which they were destroyed in such numbers. It is usually stated that they were driven into the chute and down the lane between the arms of the V, and so hurried toward the angle where they made the fatal plunge into the pen or the pit; but this is by no means an exact statement of what happened. Both buffalo and antelope are by nature curious animals, and it was the Indians' knowledge of this characteristic and their ability to play upon it that enabled them to entrap their prey. Let us see how they went to work on a hunt.

When the buffalo were near one of these old-time traps—which were called "falling places" by some tribes and are spoken of to-day as "pounds"—the first step toward capturing them was to induce them to come within the dividing arms of the V. In each tribe there were certain men who were especially skilful in this work of decoying the buffalo, either because of their great experience or by reason of some supernatural power which they had. A Blackfoot might be the possessor of an I-nis'kim—a buffalo stone—

which gave him, through some force inherent in itself, the power to call the buffalo; the member of another tribe might have some very powerful secret helper, which would aid him in his undertaking. Whatever the power he possessed, or however he had obtained it, the man who was to lead the buffalo spent a good part of the night before he made his attempt in prayer, invoking the aid of the special power on which he relied. In some cases he called in the priest to help him in his prayers, but quite as often he prayed alone, burning sweet grass and sweet pine to draw his helper to him, and also purifying himself by passing his arms and body through the perfumed smoke, and by grasping handfuls of the smoke and rubbing it over his body, arms, and legs. The members of the camp knew what was to take place the next day, and refrained from going into or even near the lodge of the man who was thus engaged in prayer.

Early in the morning, long before the dawn, the Blackfoot man arose from his short sleep and prepared for his undertaking. He neither ate nor drank, but spoke earnestly to his wives, bidding them remain within the lodge until his return, and telling them that they must burn sweet grass to the Sun and pray for his success. Then he left the lodge and climbed the bluffs toward the upper prairie where the arms of the chute were. Some men went forth naked, others carried a dress made of the entire skin of a buffalo, the head and horns arranged like a buffalo head, while the rest of the skin hung down over the wearer's back. He marched steadfastly along, speaking to no one, for he felt the solemnity of the occasion. When the caller set out, all the men and boys and many of the women of the camp followed him up on the prairie, and by twos and threes lay down behind the piles of stones which formed the arms of the chute. The caller proceeded on his way until he had come near to some herd of buffalo, whose position had been ascertained the night before. When he was near enough to be seen, yet not so close that they could clearly distinguish what he was, he began to act very strangely. He raised himself up so as to be in plain sight, then ducked out of view, stood up again and whirled round and round, hid again, and then walked to and fro, half concealed. This had not gone on long before the nearest buffalo began to stare at the man, looking for a long time in the endeavour to make out what the moving object was, and then taking a few steps toward him to get a nearer view. This attracted the attention of others of the herd, and they too began to look and to move a few steps at a time after their fellows. When the caller had succeeded in fairly attracting the attention of the nearest buffalo, he began to move slowly away in the direction of the chute. He still continued his antics, and perhaps also called to the buffalo, *Hoo, hoo, hoo, ini'uh, ini'uh, ini'uh.* As he retreated the buffalo followed, at first walking, but gradually, as they became more excited, going faster, trotting a little and then stopping to look, and at last breaking into a gallop. As they increased their speed, the man changed his pace from a walk to a trot and then to a run, and so they went on, at last at top speed, into the chute, the man running on down between the piles of stone and the buffalo in hot pursuit. As soon as they were well within the chute, however, the attention of the buffalo was distracted from the man who was leading them. For now, from behind each pile of stones which they passed, on either hand, people began to rise up and shout and yell and wave their robes. Terror took the place of curiosity; the buffalo wished to escape from these noisy and terrifying enemies; the way ahead was clear and they rushed on, heads down and tails up, at an ever-increasing speed. Yet still as they ran the people appeared just behind them on both sides, and the buffalo constantly became more frightened and ran faster, until at length, the angle of the V reached, they plunged over the cliff and down into the pen.

From the camp in the valley all the people who had not gone up on the prairie to hide behind the rock piles had gathered in the neighbourhood of the pen to await the event of the hunt. And as they sat there waiting, they could hear the first faint distant shouts of those who were frightening the herd, and then the yells coming nearer and nearer; then came the dull roar of the buffalos' tread, and then at once the leaders came pitching, rolling, falling over the cliff into the pen. All now rushed to the walls and climbed up on them so as to still further frighten the imprisoned animals. They grunted at them, making a sound not unlike the grunt of the buffalo, and by their cries and gestures strove to keep them from pressing against the walls, or from trying to climb over them. The scene within the pen, although as yet no attempt had been made to kill any of the buffalo, was already one of bloodshed. The buffalo, mad with terror, raced round and round the narrow enclosure; the strongest dashed against and knocked down the weaker, or with their horns threw them out of the way to clear a path for themselves; calves, yearlings, and those injured by the fall were thus knocked down and trampled on by their stronger fellows, or were tossed aside by their horns.

It was a case of panic in a crowd; only the strongest remained uninjured. The Indians were already swarming back from the prairie to act their part in the slaughter, but before they reached the pen, a great number of the smaller buffalo had been killed by their fellows, and only the largest and heaviest were still racing around the pen. These the men shot with their arrows as they passed them, and soon all were down, and the women entered the pen to butcher the slain. The buffalo that were not dead they despatched by breaking in their skulls with mauls. The meat after being cut up was transported to the camp and the pen was cleaned out, the skulls and bones being carried off to a little distance. And now the trees and bushes and drying scaffolds about the camp were red with great sheets of meat and white with strips of backfat, which soon began to turn brown under the hot sun and in the warm dry wind. On the ground lay many hides over which the women were working, preparing them for robes, or more completely tanning them for lodge skins or for clothing. Every one was busy and every one was happy, for there was plenty in the camp, and all day long the feast shout was heard. The fear of hunger no longer oppressed the people.

The capture of the buffalo was the work of the men, while the gathering of the fruits of the earth fell within the duties of the women. Among the agricultural tribes of the North, such as the Mandans, Rees, River Crows, Pawnees, and in ancient times the Cheyennes and some bands of the Dakotas, the women prepared the soil, and planted and hoed the corn, beans, and squashes. They gathered the crop and dried it. The women, too, dug the wild roots and gathered the berries which formed so important a part of the tribal provisions. For collecting roots they provided themselves with a stick about three feet long, curved, and sharpened at the point, shaped, in fact, somewhat like a sacking needle. This was used to unearth the roots. When berries were abundant, they visited the patches where they grew and tore off the branches of the shrubs, which they then beat over a robe spread upon the ground. The berries so gathered were dried in the sun, and, as has been said, stored in sacks for winter use. Sometimes, before they were thoroughly dry, they were pressed together in cakes to be eaten with meat like bread, but more often the dried fruit was stewed and eaten with boiled dried meat. The fruit of the wild cherry was pounded so as to crush the seed and then dried.

In many places along the flanks of the mountains the camas root grew in such abundance that it formed an important item in the subsistence of some tribes. After being dug by the women, it was subjected to a cooking process before being dried. A large pit was dug, in which a fire was built and kept up until the earth at the bottom and sides of the pit was thoroughly heated. Then the ashes were removed, and the pit lined with grass and filled with camas roots. More grass being laid on top of the roots and a little earth on the grass, a hot fire was built on top of the whole, which was kept up until the mass was cooked. This process of cooking distilled from the bulbs a brown sweet sirupy fluid, which was eagerly sought for by the children, who greedily sucked the grass with which the pit was lined. After the bulbs had been so cooked, they were removed from the pit and spread out in the sun to dry, and afterward put in sacks.

Sometimes before being dried they were pressed together in cakes to form a bread. Many other roots
were eaten.

Many of the mountain tribes peeled the bark from
certain trees at the proper season of the year, and
gathered the soft sweet inner coating which lies next
to the wood. Some tribes, like the Kutenais and
Flatheads, collected spruce gum and chewed it.

Among the tribes which lived along the larger rivers
flowing into the Pacific Ocean the great event of the
year was the arrival of the salmon on their journey up
the streams to their spawning grounds. It was during this run that the Indians secured provision for
the year, and to these people the salmon stood in just
the relation that the buffalo did to the Indians of the
plains. Shortly before the time when the salmon
might be expected, the tribes gathered at their fishing grounds, each band or family making its camp
near its own fishing stands. These stands, or favourable points for taking the salmon, belonged each to
some family, and the right to occupy each was handed
down from father to son. No family trespassed on
the stand of another, or, if this was done, it constituted a cause of offence so serious that bloodshed
might result. On the different streams different conditions made a variety of methods necessary to take
the fish, some of which have already been mentioned.
It is impossible to describe all of them.

Many salmon taken on these Western rivers are
captured by means of the dip net. This method is
still practised all along the rocky banks of the Fraser
River, in British Columbia. The river, for the greater portion of its course through the mountains, has
cut for itself a deep steep-walled channel, and the

Indian Village, Knight's Inlet, British Columbia, Showing Totem Poles.

salmon on their journey up the stream follow the shore, swimming close to the rocks, where the current is least strong, and they are measurably helped by the eddies. Along the rocky shores, at favourable points, small platforms, supported on horizontal poles, are built out over the water, on which the fisherman stands. He holds in his hand a large scoop or dip net, the pole of which is ten or twelve feet long and the hoop from two to two and one half feet in diameter. The net about the hoop is rather deep, and at intervals of six or eight inches is fastened to small wooden rings, which run freely on the large hoop of the net. A long string, passing from the back of the net up the pole to the man's hand, serves, when pulled taut, to spread the net around the hoop and keep it open; but when this string is loosened, the small rings by their weight run together at the lower part of the hoop, and the net becomes a closed bag.

When this implement is to be used, the Indian, standing on the platform, holds the pole or net in both hands, the string being drawn taut and held on the crooked little finger, and with a slow steady motion he sweeps the net with the current. If he feels anything strike it he loosens the string, the mouth of the net closes and it becomes a bag which holds whatever may be in it. It is then brought to the surface and the fish taken out, killed, and tossed on the bank. Simple as it is, this is a most effective means of taking these fish, and it requires very little skill to manipulate it. I recollect that the first time I ever used this net, I took five fine salmon in six sweeps. The salmon, nosing its way up the stream through the turbid waters, cannot see the man above it nor the approaching net, and knows of this only

6

when its nose touches the meshes, and as soon as it strikes these, the net closes about it.

The Indians begin to gather at the rivers some time before the fish make their appearance, and soon after their arrival the drying scaffolds are repaired, and the platforms, which may have been damaged by the high water of the spring freshets, are put in order. The men, while keeping always a good lookout for the coming of the salmon, hunt a little at this time, and the women are busy getting berries.

Just as with certain tribes of the Indians of the plains the buffalo hunt was preceded by religious ceremonies and the first animal taken was sacrificed to the Deity, so with these Indians of the Pacific slope, religious ceremonies and sacrifices were performed at the opening of the salmon run. The arrival of the first salmon of the season was eagerly looked forward to, and its capture celebrated with solemn rites. This first fish belonged not to its captor, but to the Deity, and as soon as caught, it was taken to the chief priest of the tribe and delivered into his keeping. A young maiden was then chosen, and, after being stripped naked and washed, cross lines of red paint, representing the meshes of a net, were drawn over her body and limbs, and she was then taken down to the river, where, while prayers were made for a great run of salmon, and for success in the fishing, the paint was washed off. This ceremony was to make their nets fortunate. Further prayers were made, the salmon was offered to the Deity, and then cut up into small pieces, one of which was given to each person present. At the conclusion of these religious rites, all were free to enter on the fishing.

The omission of this ceremony with the accompanying sacrifice was a sin which was sure to bring bad luck, and among one of the Fraser River tribes there is a story which shows how such sacrilege was punished. Just below the cañon on the Fraser, and near the town of Yale in British Columbia, a great rock or small island rises from the middle of the river, dividing the current into two streams of nearly equal volume. It is said that long ago this rock was not there.

Once, when the people gathered for the fishing, they were very hungry. All their dried fish had been eaten, their hunters had had no luck, no berries had grown that year. It was a hard time, and the people were starving. They camped here, looking for the coming of the fish, which should bring them plenty and contentment. It was a woman who caught the first fish, and she at first intended to take it to the priest, as she ought to have done, but she was very hungry, and instead of doing this she determined to say nothing about the matter and devoured the fish. For this crime the Deity changed her into a great rock and threw it into the middle of the river, where we see it now, to stand there always, as a warning to the people. Some believe that this woman, though changed to stone, can still think and feel, and that each year she is obliged to bear the pain of seeing re-enacted all about her the events in which, as a child, a young girl, and then as a mother, she had often taken part. Each year, too, she sees her people change their habits, each year perceives their numbers growing less, and the land that was once all their own passing into the hands of strangers to her race and to the soil.

Silently and with the firm endurance of her race she has borne her punishment, but the end of her sufferings is at hand. Already the thunder of the white man's blasting has shaken her, already the scream of the locomotive and the rattle of paddle wheels have sounded all about her. Some day an enterprising engineer, who wishes to improve the navigation of the Fraser, will introduce a charge of dynamite into a crevice of the rock, and the poor sinner, whose penance has surely by this time expiated her crime, will pass from the sight of men and at last find rest.

CHAPTER V.

HIS HUNTING.

IT was summer—the time of ripening berries—and the women were busy gathering the fruit and drying it for winter use. Each morning little companies of women, young and old, mounted their horses and set out up or down the stream or over the bluffs to the prairie, to the places where many berries grow. With them went some man—a husband or a close relation— who kept watch for them, while they worked, sitting on the top of some high hill where he could overlook the country, and give timely warning if any enemy should appear. Down in the brush the women were soon busy, breaking off great branches laden with ripe fruit, and beating them over a robe spread on the ground, until many had been gathered and put in the parfleches and loaded on the horses, and all the while they talked and joked and laughed.

Sometimes they might come to where a bear had been gathering berries too, and then the laughter and the talk would suddenly cease, and perhaps they came out of the bushes a good deal scared, and that day gathered no more fruit. Sometimes from the top of the hill where he sat, the man might signal that he saw people coming, and then all the women would quickly gather up their things and mount their horses and hurry toward the camp. And if the people were enemies they chased the women, and perhaps caught and killed some.

Other women went to the patches where the camas grows, and with their long crooked root diggers unearthed great piles of the roots. The pits were dug and fires built in them until the dirt all about was hot, and then the pits were lined with grass and white sage and the roots flung in and covered up. Then fires were built over the pits, and old women, staying by them, kept them burning for two or three days till the roots were cooked. Then came the uncovering, the gathering of the eager children to suck the sweet sirup from the grass and weeds, and the spreading out of the roots in the sun. When these, too, were dried and stored away for the winter, many sacks and parfleches of roots and dried sarvis berries and bull berries and pounded choke cherries were stored in the lodges.

For some time the buffalo had not been close by. The people had eaten all their fresh meat, but they still had plenty of good dried meat and backfat and tongues; so they were living well. Now, the buffalo had come again, and two young men, scouting about over the prairie to see what they could discover, had found a large herd by a little stream in a wide flat with hills all about it. They had not frightened them, nor tried to kill even a single heifer, but had gone carefully around them, and hurried back to the camp to tell the chiefs what they had seen; for these were young men of good sense, whose hearts were right.

When the people heard that the buffalo had been seen, they all talked about it and wondered what the chiefs would order to be done, and all hoped that it would be decided to chase the buffalo. When the chief learned that this food was near, he asked the priests what their opinion was about the matter—what ought to be done. And when the priests said that the signs were right, and that they would have good luck, the chief gave the order that the next day they should chase the buffalo and try to kill plenty of them. Then everybody was glad.

So the people made ready for the killing on the morrow. All the running horses were brought in and tied up, and the women had their pack horses close by the camp, where they could catch them in a little while. Every man had looked over his arms to see that his bowstring was right, that all his arrows were straight and strong, and the points well sharpened. Some young boys, who were now to make their first hunt, were excited, and each was wondering what would happen to him, and whether he would kill a buffalo, and was hoping that he might act so that his father and his relations would praise him and say that he had done well.

Many of the men prayed almost all night, asking that they might have good luck; that their horses might be sure-footed and not fall with them, and might be swift to overtake the fastest of the cows; that they themselves might have good sight to aim the arrow, and that their arms might be strong to draw the bow, so that they would kill much meat. They smoked and burned sweet grass and sweet pine to purify themselves. Other men, having told their wives to call them before the first light appeared in the east, slept all through the short night.

So now, the day of the buffalo killing had come. This morning every one arose very early, and when the time came, all the men, except those too old to ride and the few so poor that they had no horses, rode up on the prairie before the day broke. Back in the camp, many smokeholes were sending up showers of sparks, and a red glow came from some open door-ways; but in front of them the prairie was dark, and only toward the east could the hills and buttes be seen dimly standing against the pale rim of the horizon.

The eastern sky was beginning to grow light, and the stars dim; the air was cool with the chill that comes before the dawn, and there was no sound ex-cept the dull murmur of many hoof beats upon the prairie as man after man rode up and joined the others, until almost all were there and they started away.

Some of the men have saddles of antelope skin, padded with hair, but most ride without saddles, and each horse is guided by a long rawhide line, one end of which is knotted about his jaw, while the other drags on the ground. The men wear only breech-clouts and moccasins, and carry their bows and arrows in their hands. The few who use guns have the pow-der horn slung over the shoulder and a few bullets wrapped in the breechclout, but each one carries half a dozen balls in his mouth.

At first the hunters ride scattered out over the prairie without much appearance of order, some of them lagging behind, but most of them well up to the front. Yet none pass a line of men, the soldiers of the camp, who have the charge of the hunt; for to-day these soldiers are the chiefs, and everything must be done as they direct. Every one must obey them, and he who does not will have a hard time. They will whip him with their quirts, and, if he shall do something very bad, may destroy his property, cut up his lodge, break the poles, and do much harm; but every one knows how he ought to live, and if he does not observe the laws of the camp, he knows what he may expect. So the soldiers ride ahead of the hunters, slowly, keeping back those who wish to hurry ahead, giving time for those who are late or who have slow horses to catch up, so that, when the word shall be given to charge the buffalo, each one may have an equal chance to do his best.

They ride on slowly, in a loose body, some hundreds in all, going no faster than the soldiers who ride before them. Now and then, men who have been late in leaving the camp come rapidly up from behind, and then settle down into the slow gallop of the leaders. By this time the sun is rising and flooding the prairie with yellow light; the grass, already turning brown, is spangled with dew and glistens in the sunlight. The sweet wild whistle of the meadow lark rings out from the knolls, and all about the skylark and the white-winged blackbird are hanging in the air, giving forth their richest notes. Now and then a jack rabbit or a kit fox is startled from its bed in the grass by the trampling of the horses, and dashes away diagonally to right or left of the line of the advance; or a family of antelope, surprised in some hollow, race to the top of a neighbouring hill and stand there, looking curiously, until the rush of horsemen has passed out of sight.

The men do all they can to spare the horses that they wish to use for the running. Some trot along on foot beside their animals, resting an arm on the withers; others ride a common horse, and lead the runner until the moment comes for the charge; or two men may ride a common horse, one guiding it and the other leading the two runners. Mile after mile is passed over at a slow gallop until the spot where the buffalo were feeding is reached. Here the company is halted, and two or three of the soldiers creep forward to the crest of the hill and peer over. The buffalo are still there, feeding or lying down, unsuspicious of danger.

A sign from the chief of the soldiers warns every one that the time for the charge is at hand. The common horses are turned loose and the runners mounted; bows are strung, and arrows loosened in their quivers. Men and horses give signs of eagerness. The horses, with pricked ears, look toward the hilltop, while the movements of the men are quick. At another sign, all mount and ride after the soldiers, who are passing over the crest of the hill. All press to the front as far as they can, and now, instead of being in a loose body, the men ride side by side, with extended front. As they descend the slope toward the buffalo the pace grows faster, until at last the swift gallop has become almost a run, but as yet no man presses ahead of his fellows, for the soldiers hold their places; until the signal for the charge shall be given all are under restraint.

In the flat before them, scattered over the level land like cattle in a pasture, the buffalo still feed, undisturbed. Great bulls are cropping the grass on the outskirts of the herd; yellow calves run races about their mothers, or impatiently bunt them with their heads as they try to nurse; and the young cows and bulls are scattered out over the plain. All are intent on their feeding, and as yet none have noticed the dark line sweeping down toward them. In a moment, however, all this is changed: the buffalo begin to raise their heads and look, and then—either recognizing an enemy, or believing that other buffalo, frightened, are coming toward them—the herd, panic-stricken, turns away in a headlong flight. As they start, the leader of the soldiers gives the signal so long looked for. All restraint is removed. The line breaks, all semblance of order is lost, and a wild race begins, a struggle to be first to reach the buffalo, and so to have choice of the fattest animals in the herd.

Each rider urges forward his horse at his best speed. The fastest soon draw away from the main body and are close to the herd; the hindermost buffalo are passed without notice, and the men press forward to reach the cows and young animals which lead the band. The herd is split in twenty places, and soon all is confusion, and horses and buffalo race along side by side. Over the rough billowing backs of the buffalo the naked shoulders of the men show brown and glistening, and his long black hair flies out far behind each rider, rising and falling with his horse's stride. The lithe bodies swing and bend, and the arms move as the riders draw the arrows to the head and drive them to the feather into the flying beasts. It is hard to see how those who are riding in the thick of the herd can escape injury from the tossing horns of the buffalo, now mad with fear, but the ponies are watchful, nimble, and sure-footed, and avoid the charges of the cows, leap the gullies, and dodge the badger holes. In a few moments the herd is turned, and all are once more racing back over the flat from which they started; but all along where they have passed, the yellow prairie is dotted here and there with brown carcasses, among which stand at intervals buffalo with lowered heads, whose life is ebbing away with the red current that pours from their wounds, but whose glaring eyes and erect stiffened tails show that they are ready to fight to the last breath. Perhaps during the chase some hunter has driven his arrow entirely through a buffalo, and the same shaft, after passing through one animal, may have fatally wounded another. Now and again some active daring young fellow may have performed some feat of bravado as to spring from his horse onto the back of a buffalo and ride it for a while, at last killing it with his knife.

It is not long before most of the buffalo have been slain, and the men come riding back over the ground to care for the animals they have killed, each one picking out from the dead those which belong to him. These are known at once by the arrows which remain in them, for each man's shafts bear his private mark.

Meantime the women and children left in the camp have not been idle. As soon as all had eaten, and even while the men were starting out, the women began to catch and saddle the pack horses, and to fix the travois to them. Some of the larger dogs, too, were pressed into the service and harnessed to small travois. Each woman set out as soon as she was ready, following the trail made by the hunters. Most of the children accompanied their mothers, the younger ones carried along because there was no one to leave them with, the older boys and girls taken to help in the work, or going for the excitement, or because there would be many good things to eat when the buffalo were being cut up.

In this throng, which marches steadily along over the prairie, there is no pretense at discipline or order, such as prevailed among the men. It is a loose mob, strung out over a mile of prairie, careless, noisy, un-protected. It would be easy, if a little party of enemies were lying hidden behind the neighbouring hills, for them to dash down and take a dozen or fifty scalps. But the thought that this might happen occurs to no one. The women chatter and laugh with one another in shrill tones, or scold at the children or at the horses; the shouts and yells of the little boys, who dart here and there in their play, are continuous; the shrill neighing of lost colts and calling mares, mingle with the barking of the dogs and the crying of babies, the whole making a concert of high-pitched sounds which is almost deafening. All the women are riding, with their little children on their backs or on the horses before and behind them, or perhaps inclosed in wicker cages built like the frame of a sweat house on the tra-vois, and only those lads go on foot who are old enough to have escaped from woman's care, but are yet too young to hunt.

When the head of the disorderly procession reaches the crest of the hill above the killing ground a change is seen in the actions of the women and children. They call out joyfully at the sight of the carcasses, and hurry down to the flat. As the women recognise the men, scattered about skinning and cutting up the buffalo, each one hurries toward her husband or near relation to help him. The boys, excited by their sur-roundings, catch the spirit of their elders, and shoot their blunt arrows against the carcasses.

Indians are expert butchers, and it does not take long for them to skin the buffalo. The hide is drawn to one side, and the meat rapidly cut from the bones; then the visceral cavity is opened, the long intestine is taken out, emptied of its contents, and rolled up; the paunch is opened, emptied, and put aside with the liver and heart; the skull is smashed in and the brains removed, and, of course, the tongue is saved. Very likely the liver is cut up on the spot, and, after being sprinkled with the gall, is eaten raw; women and children tear off and eagerly devour lumps of the sweet white fat which clings to the outside of the intestine. All are jolly and good natured, though hard at work, and the children play merrily about. The old and steady pack horses graze near at hand, while the younger and wild ones are made fast to the horns of the dead buffalo. The camp dogs gorge themselves on the rejected portions, and gnaw at the stripped skeletons. When work on a buffalo is finished, the hide, hair side down, is thrown on a horse, on this the meat is packed; the ends of the hide are then turned up, and the whole is lashed in place by lariats. Then the party moves on to look for another buffalo killed by an arrow belonging to their lodge.

Before long, boys, girls, and women, young and old, are climbing the bluffs toward the camp, leading the laden pack horses, which not only carry heavy loads on their backs, but also drag as much more meat on the travois behind them. On reaching camp, the loads are taken off, the hides are folded up, and some of the meat is cut into thin sheets and hung on the drying scaffolds, while the choicer parts are placed in the lodge. When this has been done the hides are spread out on the ground, and the women, armed with fleshers of stone or bone, begin to cleanse them of all the flesh, fat, and blood that clings to them. All through the day the loads come into camp, and the scene is one of bustle and hard work. The men who have returned sit in the shade and talk over the incidents of the hunt; admiration is expressed for the skill and bravery of one man, while another, to whom some absurd accident has happened, is unmercifully laughed at by his fellows. If some unusual buffalo—one that is spotted or roan—has been killed, its skin is the centre of a group of the men, and the priests and doctors are asked what this portends, whether it promises good luck or bad to slayer and camp.

As evening draws on the feast shout begins to be heard from all sides, the women lay aside their tasks and prepare the evening meal. The feasters gather in various lodges, and people are constantly passing to and fro. At one or two points within the circle of the lodges, some young men and boys have built fires in the open air, and before each of these a great side of fat buffalo ribs is roasting, propped up on two green cottonwood sticks, while the lads lounge about the fire waiting for the meat to cook. When at last it is done, they shear off the long ribs one after another, and with knives and strong white teeth strip from the bones the juicy flesh.

Every one rejoices in the abundance of food. Song and dance and light-hearted talk are heard on every side, and so the night wears on.

Such was a day's hunting when were killed the buffalo, the main support of the people. The smaller animals were necessarily hunted in a different way, and deer, elk, sheep, and antelope were stalked and shot singly with arrows. If skins for war shirts are needed by a chief's wife, she tells her husband and he kills them.

In the morning early, while the first meal is being eaten, the chief directs a young man—his son or a servant—to go and bring in certain horses. The boy hastily swallows his food, and, picking up a rawhide rope, starts off for the bluffs, whence he soon returns, riding one horse and leading another, both of which he ties before the lodge. Entering the door, he soon appears again with a high-peaked saddle and a square of buffalo skin, which he straps on the led horse, and before this operation is ended, the chief comes out equipped for the hunt. He carries an old-fashioned, crooked-stocked muzzle-loading rifle, which has evidently seen long service, for its brown wood is split and bound up with thongs of rawhide put on green and allowed to dry. He slips the arm into a fringed buckskin gun case as he comes out. His balls and patches are carried in a flat beaded buckskin pouch, which hangs over the shoulder by a broad belt of dressed elk skin; the powder is in a stoppered cow's horn hanging from the other shoulder, while the caps are in a little circular rawhide box, hung from the neck by a buckskin string. Hanging from his right wrist by a buckskin loop is his quirt, the handle of polished elk horn white as ivory, while the lash is of plaited rawhide. Hitching his robe up over his shoulders, Three Suns clambers into the saddle and rides off toward the bluffs, while the younger man springs lightly on his barebacked horse and follows. Neither horse wears a bridle, but knotted about the lower jaw of each is the usual long line of rawhide by which it is guided.

The distance to the bluffs is short, and as the two ride along, Three Suns tells his companion that he intends to go to Elk River to look for mountain sheep, and explains where he expects to find them and how he proposes to hunt them. The bluffs are reached and climbed, and the men gallop swiftly over the few miles to the river.

Scattered over the yellow prairie that they are traversing are many feeding antelope, which move a little way from their path as they advance, running to the top of the nearest hills, where they stand and stamp and snort until the men have passed them. Here and there too, they see, singly or by twos and threes, buffalo bulls, but no considerable herds. Before long they draw up their horses by the side of a ravine, not far from the top of the bluffs that overlook Elk River.

Leaving the horses here, throwing down the lines so that they shall not wander, the two men crept stealthily down to a point of the bluff which commanded a view of a portion of the river bottom, and here sat down and looked over the country for game.

Before them lay a wide prospect of the valley, gray with sage, and interrupted only here and there by copses of green willow growing along the river and the wet ravines. At intervals rose groves of tall cottonwoods, whose straight gray trunks were crowned by masses of shining silvery leaves. Away to the west, the broad curves of the great river shone like ribbons of silver; in front of them its smooth waters were pale green, while to the east it was swallowed up by the gray bluffs, which there drew close together.

Scattered over the valley were many groups of antelope; down among the willows, near the river's bank, a band of elk were resting, and a few black dots were seen in the distance—bulls feeding or at rest. Near a rough rocky point of the bluff, less than half a mile above them on the bottom, were a dozen animals, whose white rumps made them look like antelope, but which were gray in color and bore great curving horns. These were sheep. It was now the

7

middle of the morning, and before long the animals might be expected to climb the rocks and lie down to rest during the warmer hours of the day. Already they were slowly feeding toward the bluffs.

Three Suns spoke a few words to his companion, pointing to the sheep and the rocks above them, and then the men cautiously withdrew to where their horses had been left. Mounting, they rode quickly to a ravine nearly above where the sheep were, and there dismounting, left their horses in a hollow well out of sight. Three Suns threw aside his robe and his gun cover, and descended the ravine toward the valley, while the boy crept to the leeward side of the bluff's point, until he had reached a position where, concealed by great stones and some low cedar bushes, he could command a view of the ridge which ran down to the valley. Here, with a sheaf of arrows in his right hand and a bow in his left, he waited and watched.

Meantime, Three Suns, hidden from view by the high ground on either side, had gone down to the level of the valley, where it was crossed by a narrow gulley, three or four feet deep, from the mouth of the ravine —in spring a water course for the melting snow, but now dry. Along this Three Suns made his crouching way. Creeping on hands and knees when the banks were low, or sometimes flat on his face, as he passed some little tributary water course which gave a view of the bottom, before long he had reached the point where the sheep should be, and choosing a spot where a thick bunch of rye grass grew on the edge of the bank, he raised his head and looked through the close-set stems. At first only the ground near to him was visible, but as his view became wider he saw, only a short distance away and between himself and the bluffs, two fat rams quietly feeding He drew back a little, crossed his two resting sticks, took a long, careful aim, and fired. One of the rams fell, while the other jumped, looked about for a moment, then trotted out of sight. Drawing back, Three Suns loaded as quickly as possible and then again raised his head, but there were now no sheep in sight. He crept on toward the point where they had been, and on ascending a little rise of ground, saw them slowly walking toward the ridge, but too far away for him to hope to reach them with his rifle. Without attempting further concealment, therefore, he walked toward the ram that he had killed, and saw the group of sheep, after stopping for a moment to look at him, turn and begin slowly to climb the bluffs.

All this the boy had seen from his hiding place, but, though he saw that the sheep had started up the point, he did not certainly know that they would come within the range of his arrows. He waited therefore, as it seemed to him, a long time, but at length he could hear the sound of stones rolling and the tread of the sheep's feet and their low calls to one another as they climbed, and presently one after another came in sight close to him, until nine stood huddled together, looking back at Three Suns. Then the boy drew his bow and sent a keen arrow through a mighty ram, just behind the shoulders, and the ram gave a great bound and rushed down the hill, and as he disappeared, another arrow struck a second ram in the throat, and he too rushed down the hill. By this time the sheep had seen the boy, and all dashed away before he could shoot another arrow, but he went down the hill, and following the blood splashed upon

the stones and dirt and grass, found first the sheep
that he had shot in the throat, and then the other.
Then he was glad, and he cut up the meat and went
for the horses and took them down to Three Suns,
and they loaded the sheep on the horses and started
to the camp.

CHAPTER VI.

THE WAR TRAIL.

INDIANS are at all times prayerful and careful in their religious observances, but they are never more scrupulous about these matters than when starting on a journey to war. Realizing that they are risking their lives, they implore divine assistance and offer in sacrifice the things which they hold most dear, giving up even parts of their bodies—slices of flesh cut from arms, breasts, and legs. A priest is asked to superintend the medicine sweat, which they take to purify themselves before starting out, and while they are in the sweat lodge, he smokes the sacred pipe and prays for these men who are about to expose themselves to danger, asking that they may return in safety to their people. While they are absent he will continue to pray for their success and welfare, and at intervals will ride about through the camp, shouting out the names of the warriors, so that they may not be forgotten by the people.

The Pawnees were obliged to offer a special burnt offering on starting to war. This was the flesh of the first deer or the first buffalo killed on the journey. Until this sacrifice had been made, it was unlawful for them to eat any fresh meat. The flesh of the antelope or of the elk might not be used in this sacrifice; to offer antelope meat, or to eat of it before the sacrifice had been made, was to commit a sacrilege and invite disaster. Under ordinary circumstances the flesh of the antelope was freely eaten, and the Pawnees had a great respect for this species as a strong animal and one possessing great endurance. It had not, however, the sacred character possessed by the buffalo and the deer.

If a war party passed any place which is sacred, presents were offered to propitiate the animals or spirits which gave the place or object its sacred character.

In their warfare two quite diverse methods were pursued. In the secret raids made for the purpose of taking horses, the parties usually were small, and relied for success altogether on their craft and adroitness. On the other hand, when an attack was to be made on an enemy's camp and a battle was in prospect, the parties were often large. In the earliest wars, when horses were few, these parties traveled always on foot; later, the large expeditions were mounted, but the small horse-stealing parties still went on foot. Two obvious reasons suggest themselves to explain this slow and laborious method of travel: Footmen can pass through any region with much less risk of detection than if they were mounted; and, further, men on foot cannot be tracked, while it is usually easy to follow the trail of horses.

If enemies are believed to be near, a war party travels by night, and at all times strives to move by hidden ways, through ravines or low places, traversing the country without leaving any sign of its passage. Thus it is not likely to be detected, except by the unfortunate accident of stumbling upon a force of the enemy. Against such misadventure it is endeavoured to provide by a thorough system of scouting. If the party consists of half a dozen or more men, one or two are always sent ahead of the main body to look over the country and report if it is safe to go on. Such scouts move with the utmost caution, and ascending to the tops of the highest hills, scan the country spread out before them with extremest care, and if the coast is clear, signal their comrades to advance. Sometimes such scouts may be disguised—as in the case of the Pawnees to represent wolves—or they may trust wholly to their craft and skill in concealing themselves, taking advantage of each hill, hollow, and ravine, until they have reached the position from which the observation is to be taken.

Certain elevated points in the debatable ground lying between the territories claimed by different tribes were regularly resorted to for this purpose. Such a point was the summit of Cone Butte, in the Judith Mountains, in Montana. Here I once came upon a shelter, built of flat slabs of the trachyte which forms the mountain's mass, large enough to contain a single man lying down, and overlooking a wide stretch of country toward the Missouri. At that time this region was a great buffalo range, and to it Blackfeet, Gros Ventres, Crees, Snakes, Crows, Assinaboines, and other tribes of the Dakotas used to resort for meat and skins. The stones which composed the front of this shelter were worn smooth by use, and the ground where the watchers had lain was deeply covered with pine boughs, some quite fresh, and others old and dry, and others still in all stages of decay. These boughs had been broken from the little pine trees that grow on the mountains' crest to make an easy resting place for the watching warrior.

The men chosen to do this scouting are persons of experience; from childhood they have been familiar with the prairie and all its signs. Thus they do not content themselves with looking for people only. They scan the stream valleys to see if among the distant animals feeding in the bottoms there are any that look like horses. The horizon is examined for a telltale column of smoke, and the movements of the birds and animals are noted. If wolves are seen sneaking off and looking back, if buffalo or antelope are running, or if the birds are uneasy, the scout draws his conclusions. But if, after a careful examination of his surroundings, nothing suspicious is seen, he signals to his comrades that it is safe for them to come on, and they join him.

As soon as the party has reached the enemy's country or suspects that enemies are near, still greater precautions are taken, and they rest and sleep during the day and travel at night. Meantime all are under strict discipline, and obey without question the orders of their leader. He is the one among them of most experience—their best warrior; no other has so much at stake as he. All are risking their lives, but he is risking reputation as well as life. His responsibility is heavy, and he feels it, and is constantly planning for the success of the expedition and praying that wisdom and acuteness may be given him. He sometimes has a certain religious pre-eminence over the others, for to him have been intrusted by the priests certain secrets of religious ceremonial. His young men obey him implicitly, treat him with the greatest respect, and so far as possible lighten his labours by carrying his burden, relieving him of work in camp, mending his moccasins, and in other ways making things easy for him.

On his part he is thoughtful of the well-being of his young men. On starting out, he is careful to see that the loads which they carry are not too heavy for their strength, and all through the journey he tries to arrange that they shall not be exposed to danger. When any occasion of unusual responsibility arises, it falls upon the leader to do the work; if any act involving great hazard must be performed, he undertakes it. He is always ready to risk his life rather than to allow his young men to go into danger. Thus the members of a war party work well together.

During their journey the warriors are careful to observe all the religious forms. It is true that those whom they have left behind them are praying for their safety, and that in their behalf the priest frequently unwraps his sacred bundle and sings his sacred songs, but they themselves do not neglect the ceremonies in which they have been instructed. At night, when they camp, the first duty to be performed is to smoke the sacred pipe and to offer up prayers. Not until after this has been done is the fire kindled or food eaten. If the party has with it a sacred bundle, which is always carried by the leader, it may be opened during the smoking and the prayers, and its contents reverently viewed. The short time which elapses between eating and going to sleep for the night is devoted by the younger men to rest and to the repairing of moccasins and clothing which has worn out, and by the leader to an exhortation to his young men. He talks to them about the dangers to which they are exposed, and urges them to be steadfast—to have a single mind. They must not rely for success on their own efforts, but must seek help from the Deity. Without his aid they can do nothing;

therefore they must implore him to pity and keep them, remembering always their own weakness. They must be considerate of other living creatures; like us, these were made by God, and he watches over and cares for them as he does for us; therefore they should not be needlessly destroyed. Besides giving this good advice, the leader tries to see that each man before he sleeps makes a special prayer for help. Before starting out in the morning the leader always makes a prayer and sacrifice, and this should be done by each one of the party. So they pursue their journey until a village of the enemy is discovered.

The camp was pitched in the valley, and from the lodges nearest the stream could be heard the soft musical rattle of the water as it hurried along over the smooth stones of the shallows. Above and below, the high bluffs came close together, but just here the valley widened, and on one side of the little river the steep hills scored by deep ravines stood a long distance from the bank, making a broad flat. At the lower end of this was a grove of timber.

The buffalo were close at hand, and in the morning all the men had gone out to chase them, and the women had followed with the travois. All day long people had been going and coming, to and from the killing ground, bringing in great loads of meat and skins. Women were still cutting up flesh and hanging it on the drying scaffolds, and spreading out hides on the ground. The camp was red with meat, and all were happy. In every lodge there was plenty. From all sides sounded the feast shout, the noise of drums, of singing, of laughter, and of talk. Sometimes, during a lull in the tumult of the camp, the sharp bark

Blackfoot Lodges

of a coyote or the hoarser howling of the big wolves gathered about some carcass, could be heard from the upper prairie, and when the camp dogs heard these sounds they barked back at their wild brothers.

The feasting and merriment continued late into the night; but at length the last of the dancers had ceased to stamp in time to the song, the last circle of feasters had been dismissed by its host, and the gamblers, who for hours had been seated opposite each other, unweariedly guessing which hand held the marked bone, had given up their game and retired to their homes. Now all the noise had died away. Even the wolves had ceased their howling and the dogs slept; only the river kept up its murmur.

The moon, which was already high in the heavens when the sun had set, was now fast dropping toward the western horizon. The Seven Persons had swung around and pointed downward, and the lodges cast black shadows that reached a long distance. It was the middle of the night. In front of the lodges were the tied horses, a few lying down, but most of them standing, with their legs a little spread apart. All were alike asleep. It was very still, and the soft murmur of the water on the stones now seemed loud, yet it was not always the same, for sometimes it grew clearer and more distinct, and again seemed to die away and almost to cease.

The time went by, and now there came from the brook once or twice another sound, as if two stones had been knocked together. It was very faint, hardly to be heard; but if the splashing of water had been joined to this faint click, it might have been thought that some one was crossing the stream, walking through the river, displacing the stones as he went. The noise

was not repeated, but a little later there was something
at the edge of the cut bank above the stream that had
not been there before—a dark object in the shadow of
a low sage brush that might have been a round black
stone. Some time passed, and suddenly a man's form
appeared erect above the bank, and with half a dozen
quick, noiseless steps, moved into the black shadow of
one of the lodges. A moment later, a second form
appeared, and then likewise disappeared. There was
another interval, and then two men walked out into
the light and passed quietly down along the line of
the lodges. They did not try to hide themselves, but
walked steadily along, disappearing for a moment, and
then coming out again into the moonlight, and if any
one had seen them, he might have thought that two
men of the camp were returning late to their homes.
At length one of them seemed to have reached his
lodge, and the other walked on a little further alone;
and then he, too, disappeared in the shadow, and did
not again step into the moonlight. And now behind
two of the lodges in the village, before which were tied
swift running horses, were crouching two young men
waiting, watching, listening to see if all was quiet.
The moon was sinking, the shadows were growing
longer, the light all about was dimmer, but it was still
clear moonlight, and one could see a long way.

Left Hand waited for a little time. With his ear
close to the lodge skins he could hear the regular
breathing of the sleepers within. Once or twice he
rose to his feet, about to step around into the light in
front of the lodge, but some slight sound from within
warned him to wait. At length he rose, and, knife in
hand, walked quickly to the horses and stooped down;
but at that moment he heard a long sigh, a rustle of

robes, and in an instant and without a sound he again vanished behind the lodge. A soft step was heard within, the door was thrown open, and a man stepped out into the light.

Left Hand was lying on the ground in the black shadow. He held his knife between his teeth, his bow in his left hand, and a sheaf of arrows in his right. There, within a few feet of him, stood an enemy unconscious of danger. It would be easy to shoot an arrow through him, count the *coup,* scalp him, and then disappear in the darkness. He wanted to kill this man, and as he lay there it was hard for him to resist the desire. But he remembered that he was the leader of a war party, and had told his young men that they were to take horses and not to kill enemies, unless they should be discovered and it should become necessary. It would not be right for him to do something that he had told his followers not to do. Besides, to kill this man might bring some of his party into danger. The man would yell, people would rush out of their lodges to see what had happened, and some one of Left Hand's young men might be caught, So Left Hand lay there and waited. The man yawned, stretched himself, and stood for a few moments looking up and down the valley. Then he re-entered the lodge and lay down, drawing his robe over him, and soon his regular breathing told that he slept.

Now Left Hand quickly arose, slipped his bow and arrows into their case, and stepping around in front of the lodges, cut loose two of the horses there and led them down the stream toward the timber. He walked on the side of the horses away from the lodges, stooping low so as to be out of sight, and the animals looked like two loose horses walking away from the camp. In the edge of the timber he met his companion, who also had taken two horses. They led the animals on through the timber and a little way down the stream, then up a ravine and onto the upper prairie. Mounting here, they rode for a mile to a low, round-topped butte. At the foot of this was a large band of loose horses, collected from the hills and herded by four young men. Left Hand said to them: "It is well, my brothers; let us go." In a moment all were mounted. The horses were started, at first slowly, but in a short time they were being hurried along at their very best speed, and before morning they were many miles away.

It was in this way that the members of a war party entered the enemies' camp, when they had set out bent only on securing plunder—the horse-stealing expedition so commonly talked of.

To thus penetrate into the very midst of the enemies' camp required not a little nerve. The successful horse-taker must be cool and ready in emergency, as well as daring. There was always a fair probability that the warrior would be discovered, for in a large camp there was usually some one moving about, or, if not, the dogs were likely to bark. If a man was recognised as a stranger, he had to act quickly to save his life. It can readily be understood that these expeditions were full of excitement and danger.

Curious things often happened to the men who entered the camp. Left Hand had once waited for some little time, watching a party of gamblers who were playing "hands" in a lodge before which was tied a horse which he greatly desired to take. At length, when he supposed all the players deeply interested, he stepped forward to cut loose the animal, but just as he was about to do so the door was lifted and two men came out and walked off a little to one side and behind the lodge. Left Hand was just stooping to cut the rope as he saw the door lifting. He stood up and walked directly up to the door, passing close to the men who had come out, who took him for some one belonging to the camp about to enter the lodge and take part in the gambling. He lifted the door as if to enter, and then letting it fall, slipped around the lodge and out of sight. Waiting until the two men had re-entered, he hurried round in front again, cut loose the horse, led it away from the lodge, mounted, and rode off. He was hardly on its back before the loss was discovered, but he made good his escape.

Four Bears, a prominent Piegan, now dead, in his young days had a friend about his own age, whom he dearly loved, and in whose company he often went to war. This young man was brave to the point of reck-lessness, and so fond of doing unexpected things from mere bravado that he sometimes got his companion into trouble, or at least frightened him very badly.

Once these young men came to a camp early in the evening, and waited near by for an opportunity to enter it without being observed. It was summer and fine weather, and the people were shouting out for feasts and going about from lodge to lodge, visiting each other; children were playing near the lodge doors, and boys and young men were chasing each other about, wrestling and shouting. Four Bears and his companion waited, but the camp did not quiet down, and they began to be uneasy, for before long the moon—now a little past its full—would rise, and then the danger of their undertaking would become much greater. At length his companion's patience became exhausted, and he told Four Bears that they must manage to get into the camp at once. He proposed that they should imitate the sportive young men of the camp, that one should chase the other into the circle of the lodges, and that there they should wrestle, separate, and then hide. The plan was carried out. They crept as near the lodges as they dared, and then, springing to their feet, raced over the plain. They did not run directly toward the camp, but drew near the lodges gradually, and at length they darted between two of them and into the circle, and then the pursuer with a shout caught the other, and they struggled and rolled on the ground. Parting again, they ran on, and for some time raced about the camp, imitating the play of the boys, trying to get a notion as to where the best horses were. Near one of the lodges, they saw a pen in which were three fine horses, and they determined that they would take these first.

After a time, people went into their homes, the fires died down, and the camp was still. The two Piegans stole to the pen and began to tear it down as noiselessly as possible. Having made an opening, they entered and caught two of the horses. The one secured by Four Bears was wild, and when he tried to lead it out of the pen it would not follow. His friend, who was waiting for him outside, looked on for a little while, and then said in his natural voice: "Why do you not get on his back and ride him out?" "Hush!" whispered Four Bears, very much frightened, "you will be heard."

"I can't help it," said the other still aloud; "I don't want to wait here all night. The moon is rising." "Do keep quiet!" said Four Bears, and, almost dead from fright, he scrambled on the horse's back. Even then the animal would not move from the pen. At this moment a man who had been aroused by the talking spoke from the lodge near by. What he said the Piegans did not know, for they could not understand his language; but Four Bear's companion called out in reply: "You had better come out here; this man is trying to take your horse." Almost in despair now, and reckless from fright, Four Bears brought down his quirt again and again on the horse's flank, and it darted noisily from the pen, through the camp, and out onto the prairie, while calls and shouts behind them showed that their flight was discovered. Four Bears used to say that he was so weak from fright that in crossing a gully he fell off his horse and for some hours knew nothing. When he came to himself, the moon, which had been just rising when they took the horses, was high in the heavens. He gathered himself up, and creeping off, made the best of his way home.

This same reckless friend of Four Bears once went across the mountains and found a Snake camp, which his party entered to take horses. The best ones were confined in a strongly constructed pen, the breaking down of which entailed a good deal of labour. His companions, as they worked, heard him grumbling under his breath, and when at last they had secured the horses he said to them: "Now, you take these horses and go off with them. I did not come here to work, but the man who owns these horses has made me work pretty hard. I am going to get even with him. You wait for me outside the camp." He went to the lodge near the pen and began to remove the pins which hold the lodge skins together over the door. Before long this awoke the man in the lodge, who, perhaps thinking that some one was playing a practical joke on him, called out something in the Snake language. The Piegan made no reply, but continued to take out the pins. At length the man rose and came to the door, and as he stepped out the Piegan drove his dagger through him, scalped him, and ran away. He joined the party, and they all got away safe to their home.

On another occasion Four Bears and his friend entered a camp to take horses. It was summer, and the weather was hot. In one lodge in the village a number of men were gambling, and, the lodge skins being raised, the two Piegans crept close to it to watch the game. After a little the friend became interested, and began to bet with Four Bears on the game, but unsuccessfully. He always guessed wrong and lost a number of wagers to his companion. Four Bears, even though he was winning, did not like to wait here, and tried to persuade the other to come away and to take the horses as intended; but the young man becoming more and more interested in the game declined to leave it. He kept betting with Four Bears and invariably lost, the man who had the bone always winning. Four Bears kept getting more and more uneasy and was trying to get away, when suddenly the young man shouted to the gambler who had the bone, "You have won every time, but you shall win no more," and with that he shot him twice with his double-barrelled shotgun, and then he and Four Bears disappeared, reaching camp in safety.

CHAPTER VII.

No one who was not familiar with the West in its early days, and with Indians as they were then, can have any conception of the difficulties and toils undergone by the members of a war party, and to have a full appreciation of them one must have followed a leader day after day for hundreds of miles over burning or frozen prairie. On foot, heavily laden, travelling from twenty to seventy-five miles a day, blistered by the fierce sun, pelted by chilling rains or choked by stifling dust, often foot-sore, without water for many hours, suffering for want of food, subject to the orders of their leader, frightened by dreams or bad omens, and in deadly peril of their lives, the sufferings of a war party, whether physical or mental, were such as might well appal any but those who had stout hearts and great singleness of purpose. Yet the Indian, trained to these severe exercises from his youth up, and coming of a race that for many centuries had been footmen, gladly endured these hardships. Even little lads, twelve or fourteen years old, or younger, used to go on these journeys, and were sometimes effective members of the party. Even if they did not actually accomplish anything themselves, they were passing through their novitiate as warriors, serving their apprenticeship, learning the features of the country so

101

that afterward they could pass through it without guide or compass, and, by watching the older warriors whom they followed, learning also the art of war as practised by their people—that art which they regarded as the noblest and most worthy of any to which a man could devote himself.

It has been said that the war parties which set out to capture horses were usually small, and that they travelled on foot. This, however, was true only of later times, after the country became more populous by the crowding into it of other tribes from the East, and by the presence of parties of white men, whether trappers, emigrants, or soldiers. In old times, sixty or seventy years ago, it was different. Then the war parties sometimes numbered a thousand men, and all were mounted. Then it was not essential to avoid observation. Such great bodies of men feared no enemy that they might meet, for their numbers were sufficient to overcome any ordinary travelling parties. Acquaintances of my own have told me of war parties which they had accompanied numbering seven or eight hundred men. Even in later times, when a war party started out to attack the settlements, they usually went in large bodies and were mounted.

In recent times it was not very unusual for a man to set out on the war path, accompanied only by his wife. Such expeditions were more often taken by newly married men, and they sometimes lasted for weeks or months and covered a wide extent of country. The woman, while not so efficient as a man would have been, was yet able to do her part on such an expedition. She was perfectly competent to gather up loose stock roaming over the hills near the camp, and to keep together these and such horses as her husband might bring to her from among the lodges of the enemy. The more difficult and dangerous work of creeping into the camp and cutting loose the better horses which were tied in front of the lodges naturally fell to the man, but having an assistant without the camp to keep together the animals which he brought, he could work much more rapidly and effectively and secure a greater number of animals.

But aside from those cases in which a woman went to war merely as a helper, occupying the place which, if she were a young man, would be that of a servant, there are many incidents recorded in Indian story where women have performed great deeds in war, and by such acts have raised themselves in the public estimation to the high level occupied by the bravest warriors. An example of this is given in a story current among the Pawnees, which is as follows:

A long time ago, once while the Skidi were on the summer hunt, some of their young men made up their minds that they would go off on the warpath. They started, travelling on foot, and went a long way up into the Sioux country. At last they came to a village, and after it was dark they went into the camp and took many ponies, and bringing them out onto the prairie, started for home, riding very fast.

One day, in the afternoon, as they were riding along, they came suddenly upon a war party of Sioux returning to the village they had just left. The Sioux charged them very bravely, and they had a battle. The Skidi killed five Sioux, but in the fight all their ponies were taken from them and nine of the ten men of the party were killed. Among the killed was the leader of the war party, and only one young man, a servant, got away. He travelled back toward the vil-

lage, and when he got there he told his people that he
was alone, that all the other members of the war party
had been killed, but that before they had died they had
killed five Sioux.

When this young man came to the village, the wife
of the leader of this war party was sitting at the edge
of the village, working on a buffalo robe, putting on it
beads and porcupine quills, so that it should be handsome and fine for her husband to wear.

When the people heard that their friends had been
killed, they all began to cry for them. The mother of
this young woman went to her where she was sitting,
and told her that her husband was dead, and that she
ought to come home and mourn for him; but when
the woman heard that her husband was dead she did
not stop to mourn, but kept on working over the robe.
She said to her mother, "Now I am nearly through
fixing up this robe, and when it is done I will go back
to the lodge." As soon as she had finished her work
she went into the village, and to the lodge where the
young man lived who had just returned. She asked
him at what place her husband had been killed and
told him to describe the spot, so that if she ever came
there she would know it, and when he spoke she listened carefully. She did not cry for her husband.

Now this young woman loved her husband and she
wanted to see him again, and in the night she got the
two fastest horses belonging to the dead man, packed
on them corn and dried meat, and on one put the buffalo robe she had just finished, and then started for
the place where her husband had been killed. She
went on and on, and after she had travelled two days
she came to the place where the dead lay. They had
been scalped and cut nearly to pieces. She looked at

Sioux Chief

her husband and saw that he had been scalped, and in her heart she determined to be revenged, and she started on the trail of the Sioux.

After three days' hard travel, she came to the top of a hill, from which she could look down and see the Sioux camp. There she hid herself in a thicket, and when night came she crept down close to it. Soon she saw in the circle of the lodges in the centre of the village a big fire, and she went into the camp and found the men and women dancing around this fire. The women were holding long poles with scalps tied to them. They were dancing in a ring, and the men danced outside of the women's circle. The woman watched the dancing until she had made up her mind which man was the leader of the Sioux. He had taken from the leader of the Skidi war party the sacred bundle that he had carried, and now had it on his back. The woman knew this bundle.

After she had seen all this, she put her robe around her, and then went in among the women dancers of the Sioux and danced with them. As they danced around in a circle, every time the Skidi woman came in front of the man who carried the bundle, she would take the robe off her head, so that the man might see her. He looked closely at her, for he did not know her, and he liked her, because she was very pretty. So they danced for a long time. About the middle of the night, the woman began to dance up to the man and to dance before him for a few minutes, and then she would go on dancing around the circle. At last everybody got tired, and they all stopped dancing and began to go to their lodges. The leader now went up to this woman and pulled her to him and took her to one side, and then tried to get her to go with him to his lodge; but the woman would not go. She would pull him toward her, and finally he went with her. Just outside the village they stopped and sat down on the prairie to talk. The man spoke to her, but she could not understand him. She did not know the Sioux language. He tried to put his arm around her, but the bundle that hung on his back was in his way, and he took it off and put it on the ground. Then he caught her and put his arms around her waist, and she put her left arm about his neck, and holding his head close to her drew her knife from her side and thrust it into his throat, over and over again. Soon the man was dead.

Then the woman stood up and took up the sacred bundle and cut off the leader's head, and went to where her horses were. She tied the head and the bundle to her saddle and started back to her village. After she had travelled for two days, she stopped for a long rest. Here she took the head from the saddle, and took the scalp off it and put it on a pole.

When the woman first came in sight of the Skidi village, no one knew who it was that was coming. She rode like a warrior, for she had the scalp on a pole and her face was painted black, and she was singing her husband's war song. The people wondered who it could be; but at last, when she got close to them, they knew who it was. Her relations had mourned her as dead, but now she came back with good news, for she brought not only a scalp, but the lost sacred bundle.

Then there was rejoicing in the village, for she wiped away the tears from parents, brothers, and sisters of the dead. Now the young warriors were afraid to meet her, for she, a woman, had taken a scalp, and they had not yet done so. After that time she was always asked to come into the councils of the braves, and she was always welcome at the old men's feasts over this sacred bundle.

It frequently happened that a small party of Indians travelling about were detected, surrounded, and surprised by a much larger body of some hostile tribe, and when this took place the destruction was often nearly or quite complete. Often, too, a small war party who were searching for a hostile camp might be discovered by the scouts of that camp, and themselves be surprised and surrounded, when their destruction was almost certain.

Every tribe that sent out parties to war has its stories of such events, sometimes telling of the total annihilation of some little band of men, and sometimes of their escape from the perils to which they had been exposed; how they were surrounded by the enemy, driven into a patch of brush or up on some high butte; how they were kept there for days; of the sufferings that they endured from hunger and thirst, and how, at length, through the prayers and the wisdom of their leader, or by the intervention of some helpful animal, or the power of some dream, they were enabled to escape from the danger, to creep through the watchful circle of their enemies, and to reach their homes in safety. Some of these stories are very curious and interesting. The Prisoners of Court House Rock, published in my book on the Pawnees, is one of these tales; another example is the escape of a war party under the leadership of Ka-min'-a-kus, chief of the Plains Crees, a tribe which, in later years, was always at war with the Blackfeet.

Ka-min'-a-kus was a great warrior and a strong medicine man. He killed fourteen Blackfeet before he lost his own life. His right eye was shot out by Low Horn in the fight when that warrior was killed.* He was twice tossed by buffalo bulls, and each time severely injured; twice thrown from his horse, each time breaking some bones; and had three scars on his right side from Blackfoot bullets. It was thought by his own people, and even by some of the Blackfeet, that he could not be killed.

Ka-min'-a-kus spoke the Blackfoot language perfectly, and often went through their camps, and even sat and gambled with them for part of the night, and the next morning a good horse would be gone, or perhaps a scalp. On one occasion a party of Blackfeet surprised him with six of his young men, and drove them out on a small point of land on a lake. The Crees dug rifle pits, and by firing from them kept the Blackfeet at bay all through the day. Night fell, dark and cloudy, and Ka-min'-a-kus told his young men to swim across the lake, leaving their guns and ammunition with him, and he would fight the Blackfeet alone. After they had gone, he ran from one hole to another, firing a shot from each, until his men had had time to get away. Then he crept out to the Blackfoot lines and began, like them, to fire at the deserted holes, and getting near to a Blackfoot he shot and scalped him, passed through the lines, and escaped. In the morning the Blackfeet found the Crees gone, and had only their own dead to look at.

Like other uncivilized people the Indians have a great respect for dreams, and believe that these foreshadow coming events. A dream often inspires a warrior to start on the warpath, and dreams which come to them

---

*Blackfoot Lodge Tales, p. 89.

during a journey to war are implicitly trusted. Thus
if a warrior dreams that he sees the bleeding bodies of
his enemies lying on the prairie, he presses forward with
renewed courage in the firm confidence that his expedition will come to a successful issue. If, on the other
hand, in his sleep he sees himself wounded or dead, or
his comrades lying dead or scalped, he loses all heart
for his undertaking and wishes to turn about and go
home.

Among all tribes stories are current which exem-
plify this feeling, and most of these stories confirm the
Indian in his belief in dreams. Some of these tales
are given in another book. The Blackfoot story of
Berry Child sets forth well the Indian's trust in dreams,
and I give it as nearly as possible in the words of the
narrator:

About seven winters before the white men built
Fort Benton, the Blackfeet were camped at the Cypress
Hills. A large party had gone to war against the
Crows, and had returned with a big band of horses
taken from their enemies.

At this time, there was in the camp a young man
who was a very brave warrior. His name was Berry
Child (Mi'na Pokau'). When he went to war, he always
had good luck and brought back horses and sometimes
a scalp or two. When the war party had started out,
this young man was away on the warpath across the
mountains, and when he came back and heard what
they had done and where the Crows were camped, he
made up his mind that he too would go to war against
them. He told the people what was in his mind, that
he intended to start off to war, and many young men
said that they would go with him, for all the people
knew that he was brave, and that he had done many

great things, and that he was always lucky in war and had a good heart, and in time of danger took care of his followers and exposed himself, while he protected them. So he had great influence in the camp, and whenever he went to war many men used to follow him.

At length, when the grass had started, the time came that he had set for leaving, and one morning his men all gathered in the centre of the camp to receive the blessing of the medicine man before they set out. They numbered many tens of warriors. When all were there, one person was still missing—Berry Child, the leader, was not present. The people wondered where he could be and why he was not with them, and they talked about it among themselves while they waited. It was not long before they saw a person coming down the bluffs toward the camp, and pretty soon they saw that it was Berry Child. He came toward the camp and came up to the circle and sat down in it. He was dressed in fine war attire of white buckskin with eagle feathers, and in his hand he held an arrow. One half of it was painted white and one half black. Its point was red.

Berry Child looked strong and brave as he stood there before the people, and his face showed that he was resolved what he should do. When every one was quiet, he stepped forward, and holding up the arrow above his head, he spoke to the young men and to all those standing near: "My fathers and you my brothers, and all you people, look at this arrow and listen to my words. Last night I had a dream. I dreamed a bad dream. I saw an eagle fly from the direction where our enemies the Crows live, and in its claws the eagle held a bunch of arrows. I saw the bird sail many times around this camp, and at last it flew past the camp and off over the prairie, and I thought it was going away. In a little while it came back and sailed three times more about the camp, and then lit upon that little hill over there, and sat there looking at its arrows, as if counting them. The eagle did not sit there long but flew away again, and when it had risen a short way in the air, it dropped one of the arrows. Then I awoke, and already it was daylight. Then I got up and went over to the hill where the eagle had been sitting, and there I found the arrow which I hold in my hand. It is not a Blackfoot arrow. You can all see that it was made by our enemies, by the Crows.

"Now, my people, this is a bad sign and I know that trouble is coming to me and to as many as go with me on this journey to war. And now I say to you young men that we are going to meet great danger, and as many of you as fear death should not follow me. For myself, I intend to go to war, as I have said I would do, but I ask no one to come with me. Let each man decide for himself what he will do. I cannot advise you to stay at home or to follow me. As for me, while my body is strong, and while my eyesight is clear and good, and while there is no white hair in my head, I would like to die in battle. I have many young brothers growing up to take my place. They will care for my father and mother when they are old. Brothers, some of you have no close relations, no one to help your old people if you should die. I should not like to have you lose your bodies on my account, nor that your old people should mourn for you, and should starve if you do not come back from war. Think of these things, and make up your minds what you will do."

When he had finished speaking, all the people began to talk at once, and some said one thing and some another, but all thought that the arrow the eagle had dropped was a bad sign, and that the Sun had sent the bird to warn the party not to start. Still, some thought that the sign meant danger only to the leader. But all the young men of his party said that they were willing to follow Berry Child to war. So they started, against the will of their people, for they were resolved to follow their young leader.

The war party went on, travelling southwest until they came to the Missouri River. Here they killed some buffalo, and it was decided to camp for a while and rest. So far all had gone well, and the young men were in good heart after their feast.

The second chief of this party was named Spotted Wolf. He was a middle-aged man, and was known to be powerful with dreams. One night, they all lay down to sleep, and the next morning each man had a strange dream to tell. Some had dreamed sad things and some funny things, all different. When Spotted Wolf told his dream to the party, he said: "I dreamed that I saw this whole party lying on the prairie dead and scalped, and from where we lay all killed together, I saw a stream of blood flowing on the ground down the hill. This was a strong dream, for I saw it all as plain as I see you now, and I knew each man as he lay dead. My opinion is that it is best for us to turn about and go home, for my dream has told me that there is too much danger before us."

The warriors talked about this for some time, and some thought that it would be best to go home, and some wanted to go on, but at length they all decided to go a little further. The next night Spotted Wolf dreamed again, and in the morning he told his dream.

"Brothers," he said, "now I know for certain that something bad is going to happen to us. I dreamed that I was going along, and I came to a spring and bent down to the water to drink. The water was still, and I saw myself in it; and when I saw my head, it was bare and all bloody, there was no hair on it. It had no scalp. Trouble is coming for us, and I think we had better go back to our own country. Whatever the rest may decide, I shall go back."

Then Berry Child said: "Brothers, I want to see the end of this, and I am going on. If any of you will follow me, you can come on; if any wish to go back, they can go."

The party divided here, the larger number going back to the Blackfoot camp, while twenty-six men followed Berry Child, determined to see the end.

For many days the party travelled on through the mountains, and when they came to the forks of the Musselshell, they saw fresh signs of enemies, but they could not find their camp. They went on, until they came to Deer Creek and the Yellowstone, and here they found a camp where the Crows had been, but from which they had moved the day before, so that now they could not be far off. While they were waiting here, one of the party was bitten by a rattlesnake and could go no further on foot, so they gave him some food and left him hidden here, intending to come back that way and take him with them.

When they had travelled up Deer Creek half a day's journey, they were seen by the Crows, and a large party of warriors attacked them. They made a brave stand, but the Crows were too many, and drove them into a patch of cherry brush in the valley, and surrounded them. The main Crow camp was not far off, and when the news came to it, the whole Crow village moved down and camped all about the Blackfeet.

The next morning the Crow chief stood out in front of the patch of brush and spoke to the Blackfeet in signs, telling them that they had better give themselves up, and that if they would do so the Crows would make friends with them. "It is useless for you to fight," he said. "You are twenty-five brave men, but we are three hundred lodges of people. Give yourselves up and be our friends." Then Berry Child stepped out of the brush, and in signs answered the Crow, saying: "It is not the custom of the Blackfeet to surrender and make friends in battle. I have come to war, to fight, and, if I must, to die. I am here, and I am willing to die. Here is my body. It waits for you to count *coup* on it. Here is my scalp, who will come and take it? I have come to war, not to make friends."

Then all the Crows got ready and attacked them. The Blackfeet stood their ground, fighting bravely till near sundown; but the Crows kept charging them in great numbers, and in the afternoon the last of the twenty-five was killed. Not one escaped. The man who had been bitten by the snake got better, and he alone returned to the Blackfeet camp.

It is impossible for us who live commonplace, humdrum lives of a civilized community to form any adequate conception of the variety and excitement of the life of a young man who was constantly going on the warpath. The barest enumeration of the odd circumstances and thrilling occurrences which took place in a single tribe of a brave, warlike nation would fill many volumes. Such a recital would present many examples of reckless hardihood almost beyond belief, cases where men have mingled with the members of a hostile camp, taking part in their gambling games, like Ka-min'-akus, or have given themselves over to the enemy to be slain, as did Owl Bear and Running Chief, or, through kindness of heart or mere good nature, have undertaken some very dangerous expedition, like that which the Bridled Man entered into for the sake of his wife. This story, as given by the Piegans, is as follows:

In the Piegan camp there was a man whom they called A'yĕs-kwō-yē-pĭs'ta, which means he is bridled. His lips had been eaten away, and across his face, covering his mouth, he used to wear a piece of cowskin, to hide the scar. This is what gave him his name.

This man had a good heart. He was always doing kind things. Sometimes, when he was the last to leave the camp, he would see little puppies which had been left behind to starve, and would pick them up and carry them in his robe to the next camp, and nurse and feed them until they were strong enough to go about by themselves. He was a very brave man. One time when he went to war, he found a camp of Snake Indians. When he had found them, he said to his party: "Well, now, my young men, we are looking for death, and there is the enemy. I intend to charge this village and give them battle." They charged the village and a great fight followed, and they defeated the Snakes and got them frightened and running, and they captured a large number of women. He told his men not to kill the captured women. They also captured the village and many children, and everything that the Snakes had.

9

When the battle was over, they started back with the horses and other plunder that they had taken, and took the women with them. The Bridled Man selected a wife for himself from among these women. While he was in his own camp, he could not get a wife. No woman would marry him, he was so ugly. When he reached his camp, he had many scalps and many prisoners, and many strange things that he had taken from the enemy. So he was much respected, and everybody looked up to him.

He started off on another war trip, and took with him his captured wife. The woman used to guide him about through the country, and tell him where the tribes of her people were likely to be at each season of the year. They went down south into a strange country and there found a camp of people. He said to his followers, "Now we will have to give this people battle, and see what success we will have here." Before he had started on the warpath he had made himself a bone dagger, and was armed with this and a shield and a stone axe. The Piegans charged the village, and the Bridled Man showed great bravery. He rushed on the enemy and killed them with the bone dagger, and pounded them down with his battle-axe. The enemy tried to shoot him, but he protected himself with his shield. While this fight was going on, a number of the enemy rushed on him, and caught hold of him and threw him down, and he was under them on the ground squirming and stabbing and kicking, and at last he got up and away from them. During the battle the voice of Bridled Man could be heard calling out: "Take courage, my young brothers; take courage! There are many of our young brothers growing up who can take our places if we fall in battle."

The Piegans conquered the village. They captured a great many women and children, and his young men killed some of the women and children secretly; but this was against the Bridled Man's wishes. This did not please him, and he did all he could to stop it. When they got back to the main camp, a great feast and a war dance were given in honour of the Bridled Man.

After they had been back at their camp for some months, his wife began to beg her husband to take her back to her people. She used to say to him: "My father and the people that I belong to are great chiefs. If you will take me back to them, no harm will come to you." Her husband would answer: "I do not like to do this. I have done so much harm to your people that it will be hard for them to forgive it. I have defeated them in battle, have taken their camps, have scalped their warriors and captured their women and children. It would be hard for them to overlook all this." The woman would say: "No, I feel certain that I am right. My father and my brothers are the heads of the camp, and they love me dearly. I know that what I say will be so."

After she had coaxed and teased him for a long time, at last he said to her: "Well, let it be so. I will take you to your people, although I know that I shall not get back here. I shall not survive. I shall be killed." When he had made up his mind to start, he invited many of the head men of the camp into his lodge and spoke to them, saying: "My young people, there is one thing I want to tell you. It is a hard thing for a man to be too good-hearted. For a long time this woman has been asking me to take her home to her own people. I have promised to do so, and I do not wish any of you to object to it or try to stop me. I am going to do what she asks, but I do not expect to return here. I expect to be killed."

He told his wife to get ready, and that they would go. While they were making ready to start, the Bridled Man made himself a cowskin coat, with large parfleche cuffs to it which reached up to his elbows, and in these cuffs he sewed a lining, and between the lining and the cuff he put a knife and sewed it there, but his wife did not know it was there. His other knife he put in his belt in its usual place.

At last they were ready, and they started on foot and travelled many days. At length the woman said to her husband: "When we get on top of this mountain, looking southeast, you can see, way off, a river. At this time of the year, all my people come and camp on this river. There they dig camas and bitter root, and gather service berries to dry them." When they got on the hill and looked over, there, far off they could see the river. By this time their moccasins were nearly worn out. They travelled on toward the river, and when night overtook them they camped. When they lay down to rest the man said to his woman: "I think I hear something in the distance. Do you not hear it?" The woman said, "No, I hear nothing." He said: "I think I hear a drum beating in the distance. Now, you listen." The woman listened, and then said: "Yes, I think I do hear a drum beating; but never mind, we will sleep here to-night." But the man said: "No, if that is a drum, the camp is close by; we had better go there to-night." So they packed up and started. They went on, and when they had come close to the camp, they could hear drums beating for a dance, and the talking and laughter of the people up and down the river for a long way; and they could tell that there were many people camped here on this river. The man said: "Well, we are here. I am satisfied that I shall not see to-morrow's sun. You have brought me to your country to get killed. It is always a foolish man's way to listen to a woman." The woman said: "No, do not be uneasy. My father is the great chief of this camp. You wait here for me. I will go into the camp. I will look through the lodges until I come to where my father or brothers are, and if I find them, I will tell them that you are here and I will come back with them and get you. I know that they will not hurt you." Her husband said: "All right; I will wait here. Come back to this place. I will not run away. We will see what is going to happen." She said: "I will go to where this great dance is, and if my father is in the camp, he will be there. He will be sitting in the back end of the lodge, where the chief sits."

The woman went off, and the Bridled Man waited a long time for her to come back. He fell asleep, and then woke up. At last he got tired of waiting for her, so he thought, "I will go down there and see what is the matter." Before he started, he untied the string of his parchment cuff, and tried his knife to see if it slipped out and in easily. He went into the camp and right to the dancing lodge, where the drum was beating. When he got there, he found that they were giving a great war dance. They had made a very big lodge, and when he came close to it, he had hard work to get to the door on account of the great crowd of women and children standing around. He pushed his way through these people toward the lodge. He had his bow strung, and had taken his knife from the back of his belt and put it in front, where he could easily get at it if he needed it. When he got to the door of the dance lodge, he went in. He walked right along the row of dancers to the back of the lodge where the chiefs were sitting. In the middle, in the back of the lodge, was a back-rest leaning against the lodge poles. There sat the head chief. He walked up to this man, moved his legs apart, and sat down right in front of him and between them. He reached down and took the chief's hands, and folded them in front of his own body. The dancers all stopped and sat down. The drum ceased beating. It became still, and every one turned his eyes on the stranger who had just come in.

The people talked among themselves, but he could not understand what they were saying. Two men who sat at the opposite end of the lodge, one on either side of the door, got up and came toward him. They had nothing on save breech-clouts, and in their right hands daggers. These men caught hold of the Bridled Man, one by each hand. He braced himself and held stiff, but they dragged him along and he slid over the ground toward the door. When they had got him to the door, he pulled away from them and walked quietly back to the chief, spread his legs apart, and sat down in front of him, and put the chief's arms around his own body as before. The two soldiers again came up to him. This time they snatched off his blanket, and took his bow and arrows away from him. Again they came up to him, singing, and, seizing him by the wrists, pulled him up to his feet, and dragged him toward the lodge door. By this time there was a great uproar outside and at the door, people trying to get out and go away, for they knew that killing would take place as soon as he was taken outside. Other people wanted to get in and see what was going on. There was crowding and confusion. When the soldiers got the Bridled Man close to the door, he jerked away from the right hand man, struck the other and knocked him away, and walked back and sat down as before. He kept this up until he had done it four times. The chief sat there, saying nothing. He neither tried to encourage his men nor to stop them. He did not move nor speak. He paid no attention.

The fourth time that they dragged him to the door, his bridle was torn off his face. He jerked loose from the men, folded his arms, and walked back to the chief. When he got to him, he bent down, took hold of the chief's arm, lifted it up, and drawing the knife from his cuff, thrust it several times into the Snake chief's side. Then he gave the Piegan warwhoop, and started for the door, jumping at every man he saw. The dancers started up in terror and rushed for the door. He was right among them, stabbing and cutting and giving the warwhoop every time his knife came down, and all the time getting nearer to the door. When he got outside, the crowd started to run, but they fell over each other, and he was among them in the darkness, stabbing every one he could reach. When the people had cleared away from in front of him, he started to run toward the river.

Opposite this lodge, and on the river bank, was a point of tall pine trees, and one had fallen down into the river and reached part way across it. He ran on to this point and out on the fallen tree, and as he ran he made the chattering noise that a pine squirrel utters. When he got to the end of the tree, he jumped into the water and so got across the river, and made his way up on the mountain and hid himself.

He stayed there all the next day. The next night he went back to the camp again, to see if he could steal into a lodge and find moccasins and some clothes to wear. He went into different lodges, trying to gather up what he could lay his hands on. He could find nothing to cover himself with, so he went to where a couple were sleeping, jerked the robe off them, and ran out of the lodge. In another lodge which he entered, a man was sleeping with moccasins on, and he took them off him. He found some dried meat, and now, as it was getting toward morning, he crossed the river, went up to his hiding place, and there waited again all day.

That night he returned to the camp, and went into a lodge. At the head of a bed where a young man was sleeping, he found a quiver of arrows and a bow, and he took them. When he went out of the lodge and started down toward the river, there he saw a person sitting. She had gone down after some water. He walked up to her, put one hand over her mouth, and caught her around the waist and started off with her. He did not speak to her. When he got her away from camp, he kept on travelling with her. He never stopped and never spoke. When daylight came, and she saw that it was a strange Indian, she was afraid of him. He told her by signs, "I am going to take you with me. Come on." She did not resist in any way, but went with him. When they camped that night, the man was very tired. They lay down to sleep for the night, and he went to sleep at once. When he awoke, he found that the woman was gone. So he kept on travelling, and returned to his people.

It was learned afterward, during a friendly meeting

with the Snakes, that he had killed twenty of those people in his rush for the door.

Although the Indian, as a rule, shows no mercy in his warfare, killing alike men and women and children, and acting as if his motto were "Slay and spare not," yet he can take pity, sometimes displaying a magnanimity hardly to be looked for in a savage, and foregoes the opportunity to rid himself of an enemy, even when he can do so without danger to himself. Instances of such generosity are not often witnessed in the excitement of battle, but that they do occur is shown by examples such as those given in the stories of Comanche Chief, Lone Chief, and The Peace with the Snakes, which I have recounted in earlier volumes. In these particular instances the feeling which induced the chiefs to spare the men whose lives were in their hands appears to have been respect for their bravery. They wished to give the strongest possible proof of their admiration for this quality. Other stories tell of similar instances where the motive seems to have been mere good nature, and often the release of captives taken in war was prompted by kindness of heart, the prisoner being supplied with arms, food, and a horse, and then taken off to a distance from camp and dismissed to go to his home.

Sometimes fear might cause a man to spare an enemy's life. If the latter was thought to have very strong "medicine," the man in whose power he was might deem it prudent to treat him as a friend, rather than to run the risk of offending the protecting spirit whose power was so great.

On the other hand, defeat, or the loss of some popular man, might lead the victors to torture the captive man, who was then sacrificed in revenge for the injury inflicted by his tribe on the enemy. I have elsewhere spoken of the sacrifice of the captive by the Skidi, but this, it will be remembered, was not done from any warlike feeling. It was a purely religious ceremony. The Rees, while they never, so far as known, sacrificed the captive in the same way as the Skidi, nevertheless had a similar custom, though it was a mere ceremony, and did not involve loss of life or even suffering to the captive. Among some other tribes a captive was occasionally offered to the Sun or principal deity, rarely being killed, but usually being tied securely and left to perish alone.

CHAPTER VIII.

In the historic period, the Indian has always been a warrior. Urged on by the hope of plunder, the longing for reputation, or the desire for revenge, he has raided the white settlements and made hostile incursions against those of his own race; and each war party that set out endeavoured to injure as much as possible the enemy it attacked. As each woman might fight or be a mother of warriors, and as each child might grow to be a warrior or a woman, women and children were slain in war as gladly as men, for the killing of each individual was a blow to the enemy. It helped to weaken his power and to strike terror to his heart.

But the Indian has not always been a warrior. Long ago, there was a time when war was unknown and when all people lived on good terms with their neighbours, making friendly visits, and being hospitably received, and when they in turn were visited, returning this hospitality. The Blackfeet say that "in the earliest times there was no war," and give a circumstantial account of the first time that a man was killed in war; the Arickaras have stories of a time when war was unknown, and tell about the first fighting that took place; and in like manner many of the tribes, which in our time have proved bravest

125

Crooked Hand, a Pawnee Brave

and most ferocious in war, tell of those primitive days before conflict was known.

I have elsewhere* given my reasons for believing that previous to the coming of the whites there were no general or long-continued wars among the Indians, because there was then no motive for war. No doubt from time to time quarrels arose between different tribes or different bands of the same tribe, and in such disputes blood was occasionally shed, but I do not believe that there was anything like the systematic warfare that has existed in recent years. The quarrels that took place were usually trivial and about trivial subjects—about women, about the division of a buffalo, etc. Real wars could have arisen only by the irruption of one tribe into the territory of another, and the land was so broad and its inhabitants so few that this could have occurred but seldom.

It is difficult for us, with our knowledge of improved implements of war, to comprehend how bloodless these early wars of the Indians must have been. A shield would stop a stone-headed arrow, and at a slightly greater distance a robe would do the same. Their stone-headed lances were adapted to tearing and bruising rather than to piercing the flesh, and their most effective weapon was no doubt the stone warclub, or battleaxe, which was heavy enough, if the blow was fairly delivered, to crush in a man's skull. In those old days, we may imagine that in many, if not in most, of the battles that took place, the combatants, however anxious they may have been to kill, were forced to content themselves with beating and poking each other, giving and receiving nothing

---

*Blackfoot Lodge Tales, p. 242.

more serious than a few bruises. Those who have witnessed fights in modern times between considerable bodies of Indians armed with iron-pointed arrows, knives, and hatchets, will remember how very trifling has been the loss of life in proportion to the numbers of the men engaged. Such battles, as I have elsewhere shown, might go on for half a day without loss of life on either side, but when one party acknowledged defeat and turned to run, the slaughter in the pursuit might be considerable.

In these wars between different tribes, the greatest losses usually occurred when one party was surprised by another, the attacking party killing a number of men at the first onslaught, and perhaps in the ensuing panic. If, however, those attacked rallied and turned to fight, the assailants, unless they greatly outnumbered their enemy, often drew off at once, satisfied with what they had accomplished in the surprise.

The story of the last great fight which took place between the three allied tribes of Pawnees and the Skidi tribe, just previous to the latter's incorporation into the Pawnee nation, is an example of this, and has never been told in detail. It gives a good idea of one view of Indian warfare, shows that they had some notions of strategy, and also brings out in strong relief the common sense and benevolence of the Kit'ka-hah-ki chief. The story was told me many years ago by an old Chaui', substantially as given below. He said:

It was long ago. At that time my father was a young man. I had not been born. Many years before, the three tribes of Pawnees had come up from the south, and had found the Skidi living in this country. Their villages were scattered along the Broad River (the Platte) and the Many Potatoes River (Loup).

There were many of them, a great tribe. But there were many more of the Pawnees than there were of the Skidi.

When our people first met the Skidi, we were friendly; we found that we spoke a language almost the same, and so we learned that we were relations—the same people—so we smoked together and used to visit each other's villages, and to eat together. We were friends. But after a while, some of the Skidi and some of the Chaui´ got to quarrelling. I do not know what it was about. After that there were more quarrels, and at last a Skidi was killed; and after that the people were afraid to go near the Skidi village, and the Skidi did not come near the Chaui' village for fear they might be killed.

One time in the winter, a party of men from the Chaui' village, which then stood on the south side of the Broad River, just below the place of the Lone Tree (now Central City, Neb.), crossed the river to hunt buffalo between the Platte and the Loup. While they were killing buffalo, a war party of the Skidi attacked them and fought them, and killed almost all of them. Some of the Chaui' got away and went back to their village and told what had happened, and how the Skidi had attacked them.

Now at this time the Chaui' and the Skidi tribes were about equal in numbers, and the Chaui' did not feel strong enough to attack the Skidi alone. They were afraid, for they knew that if they did this, it might be that the Skidi would defeat them. The Kit'ka-hah-ki tribe were living on the Much Manure River (Republican), and the Pita-hau-i'rat on the Yellow Bank River (Smoky Hill). To these two tribes of their people the Chaui' sent the pipe, telling them what had happened, and asking them for help against the Skidi. Each of the tribes held a council about the matter. All the best warriors and the wise old men talked about it, and each one gave his opinion as to what should be done; and they decided to help the Chaui'. The two villages moved north and camped close to the Chaui' village, and all the warriors of all three tribes began to get ready for the attack. By this time it was early summer, and the Platte River, swollen by the melting of the snows in the mountains, was bank full—too deep and swift to be crossed either by wading or swimming. So the women made many "bull boats" of fresh buffalo hides and willow branches, and in these the Pawnee warriors crossed the stream. The main village of the Skidi was on the north side of the Loup River, only about twenty miles from that of the Chaui'. The crossing of the Pawnees was accomplished late in the afternoon, and a night march was made to a point on the south side of the Loup, several miles below the Skidi village.

Here they halted and distributed their forces. One hundred men, all mounted on dark-coloured horses, were sent further down the stream, and were told what to do when morning came. The remaining warriors hid themselves, half in the thick timber which grew in the wide bottom close along the river, and half in the ravines and among the ridges of the sandhills above this bottom. Between the sandhills and the timber was a wide, level, open space. The Pawnees were so many that their lines reached far up and down the stream.

When daylight came, the one hundred men who had been sent down the stream came filing down from the prairie one after another. Each man was bent down on his horse's neck and covered with his buffalo robe, so that at a distance these one hundred riders looked like one hundred buffalo, coming down to the water to drink. The spot chosen for them to pass could be seen from the village of the Skidi. In that village, a long way off, some one who was watching saw these animals, and called out to the others that buffalo were in sight. It was at once decided to go out and kill the game, and a large force of Skidi set out to do this. They crossed the river opposite the village, and galloped down the bottom on the south side. In doing this, they had to pass between the Pawnees who were hidden in the timber and those in the sandhills. They rode swiftly down the river, no one of them all suspecting that anything was wrong; but after they had passed well within the Pawnee lines, these burst upon them from all sides and charged them. Attacked in front, on either side, and in the rear—taken wholly by surprise, and seeing they were outnumbered—the Skidi tried to retreat, and scattering, broke through the lines wherever they could and ran, but all the way up that valley the victorious Pawnees slaughtered them as they fled. They took a good revenge, and killed more than twice as many of the Skidi as those had of the Chaui'.

At last the Skidi who were left alive had crossed the river and reached their village, and had told their people what had happened, and how they had been attacked and defeated, and had lost many of their men. All the warriors who were left in the village armed themselves, and came to the river bank to meet the Pawnees when they should cross, determined to die there fighting for their homes.

When the Pawnees reached the crossing, a part of

them wanted to ford the river at once and attack the Skidi village and kill all the people in it, so that none of the Skidi should be left alive. The chiefs and head men of the Pita-hau-i'rat and the Chaui' wanted to do this, but the Kit'ka-hah-ki chief said: "No, this shall not be so. They have fought us and made trouble, it is true, but now we have punished them for that. They speak our language, and they are the same people with us. They are our relations, and they must not be destroyed." But the other two tribes were very bitter, and said that the Kit'ka-hah-ki could do as they liked, but that they were going to attack the Skidi village, burn it, and kill the people. For a long time they disputed and almost quarrelled as to what should be done. At length the Kit'ka-hah-ki chief got angry, and said to the others: "My friends, listen to me. You keep telling me what you are going to do, and that you intend to attack this village and destroy all these people, and you say that the Kit'ka-hah-ki can do what they please, but that you intend to do as you have said. Very well, you will do what seems good to you. Now I will tell you what the Kit'ka-hah-ki will do. They will cross this river to the Skidi village, and will take their stand by the side of the Skidi and defend that village, and you can then try whether you are strong enough and brave enough to conquer the Kit'ka-hah-ki and the Skidi, fighting side by side as friends." When the Chaui' and the Pita-hau-i'rat heard this, they did not know what to say. They knew that the Skidi and the Kit'ka-hah-ki were both brave, and that together these two tribes were as many as themselves. So they did not know what to do. They were doubtful.

At last the Kit'ka-hah-ki chief spoke again, and

10

said: "Brothers, what is the use of quarrelling over this. The Skidi have made trouble. They live here by themselves, away from the rest of us. Now let us make them move their village over to the Platte and live close to us, so that they will be a part of the Pawnee tribe." To this proposition all the Pawnees, after some talk, agreed.

They made signs to the Skidi on the other bank that they did not wish to fight any more, they wanted to talk now, and then they crossed over. They told the Skidi what they had decided to do, and these, cowed by their defeat and awed by the large force opposed to them, agreed to what had been decided.

The Pawnees took for themselves much of the property of the Skidis—many horses. This was to punish them for having broken the treaty. Also they made many of the Skidi women marry into the other Pawnee tribes, so as to establish closer relations with them. Since that time the Skidi have always been a part of the Pawnee nation.

Cunning is matched with cunning in the following story, told me by the Cheyennes:

About the year 1852 the Pawnees and the Cheyennes had a fight at a point on the Republican River, where there was a big horseshoe bend in which much timber grew. A war party of each tribe was passing through the country, and the scouts of each discovered the other at about the same time, but neither party knew that its presence had been detected. The Cheyennes, however, suspecting that perhaps they had been seen, displayed great shrewdness. They went into the timber, built a large fire, ate some food, and then cut a lot of logs, which they placed by the fire and about which they wrapped their blankets and robes, so that they looked like human figures lying down asleep. Then the Cheyennes retired into the shadow of a cut bank and waited. Toward the middle of the night, after the fire had burned down, the Pawnees were seen coming, creeping stealthily through the brush, and when they had come close to the fire, they made an attack, shooting at the supposed sleepers, and then charging upon them. As soon as they were in the camp and were attacking the dummies, the Cheyennes began to shoot, and then in their turn charged, and in the fight which followed eighteen or nineteen Pawnees were killed.

The old Cheyenne who told me this, chuckled delightedly, as he remarked, "The Cheyennes often laugh at this now."

The Indians set a high value on life, and do not willingly risk it. Warriors and chiefs always tried to keep those under their command from exposing themselves, for it was a disgrace for the leader of a war party to lose any of his men. It was their policy to inflict the greatest possible injury on the enemy with the least possible risk to themselves. They aimed to strike a telling blow, and before the enemy had recovered from the surprise to put themselves out of the way of danger. Their war was one of ambuscades and surprises, and having been educated to this method of fighting, they were not at all fitted to carry on battles in which there was steady and open fighting. In light cavalry tactics or guerilla warfare they excelled, but in the early days they could not face the steady fire of men at bay. Under such conditions they became unsteady and soon broke. The fact that they have been brought up to fight on a different principle from the white man has gained for Indians the reputation of being cowards, but in later years the warfare of more than one tribe of plains Indians has demonstrated that when they have learned the white man's way of fighting, they are as brave as he.

Notwithstanding all that has been said, desperate battles were now and then waged between Indian tribes, fights which, for ferocity and bravery, perhaps equal anything that we know of in civilized warfare. The last considerable fight which took place between the Piegan tribe and the allied Crows and Gros Ventres of the Prairie was such an one. The story of this fight, as I give it below, is compiled from the narratives which I took down in the year 1891 from the lips of three men who were engaged in the battle, and I have no doubt that it is a fairly accurate account of the events of the day. The occurrence is interesting from the completeness of the victory and the great number of the slain on the defeated side. Aside from this, the account, as here given, is full of characteristic Indian forms of thought, and, in the matter-of-fact way in which its bloody details are related, it furnishes an excellent illustration of the point of view from which Indians look at war and its events.

It was toward the end of the summer, when the cherries were ripe—twenty-four years ago (1867)—that this fight took place. Wolf Calf was already old. Mad Wolf was a young man just in his prime. Raven Lariat was a full-fledged warrior. Wolf Tail was very young; he had not yet taken a woman to sit beside him.

All the Piegans except Three Suns' band—in all perhaps two thousand lodges—were camped about twenty miles east of the Cypress Hills. On the day before the fight, early in the morning, a single Piegan had been travelling along near the Cypress Hills, on his way back from a journey to war. He had only one horse. As he was riding along, he passed near a large camp of Crows and Gros Ventres. They saw him before he did them and chased him, but he rode in among the pines and got away from them, and reached the Piegan camp in safety. He gave the alarm, telling the people what he had seen, but they did not believe him. They said: "This cannot be true. If two people had said it, or three, we would believe it, but this man is just trying to frighten us." So they did nothing.

The man who at this time was the chief of the Piegans was one of those who made the first treaty with the whites. His name in that treaty was Sits in the Middle. His last given name was Many Horses. On the day when the fight took place, early in the morning, before it was light, before they had turned loose the horses, the old chief got up and said to his wife, "Saddle up, now, and we will go out to where I killed buffalo yesterday, and get some meat and the brains." His wife saddled the horses and they started, and had ridden quite a long way out on the prairie before it became plain daylight.

About this time Mad Wolf, as he lay in his lodge, heard a man on a little hill just outside the camp shouting out: "Everybody get up and look. A great herd of buffalo is coming this way." Mad Wolf sprang out of bed and rushed out, naked as he was, and a few others with him, not many. They saw the buffalo coming. It was a great sight, a tremendous throng as far as you could see, coming toward the camp, but still far off. A man named Small Wolf took a few young men and started out toward them, to kill some. After a little time a man, who stood there on the hill looking, said:

"Hold on. Perhaps those are not buffalo. Are there not some white animals among them? They may be horses." He called to some one to bring him a field glass, and when he had looked through it, he said: "Oh, it is just a multitude of people coming. They are Crows and Gros Ventres." Then they all shouted in a loud voice, for most of the people were still in bed: "Get out here! The Crows and Gros Ventres are coming! Take courage!"

A war party of Piegans had been out, and, returning, had camped close to the main Piegan camp; also some people had gone out the night before to camp close to the buffalo, so as to make a run early in the morning. The enemy attacked these outlying parties first, and drove them, killing some, and the people in camp heard the shooting. About this time, Small Wolf came running into camp, gasping for breath, and called out: "Come quick and help us; my party is almost overcome!" By this time, too, the enemy had run off about half the band of horses belonging to Many Horses.

In those days the people were not well armed. Some of them had guns, but most had only bows and arrows and lances and heavy whips.

The Piegans had run to drive their horses into camp, and as they came in, they began to get ready to go out and fight. The head men tried to persuade the first ones to wait, so that all should start out together, but some were in too great a hurry to wait.

By this time the enemy were close to the camp and on a little ridge. There were women and boys in the party. The Piegans had begun to fight, but not very many had yet gone out. A Piegan, named Screaming Owl, whose medicine was very strong, was the first man shot. He was hit in the belly with a ball, but it did not go into his body.

There was a Gros Ventre chief who was very brave. He seemed to be going everywhere among his people, encouraging them and fighting bravely himself. Some Piegan shot this man, breaking his leg above the knee, and he fell. Then all the Crows and Gros Ventres cried out in a mournful way that the medicine had been broken, but still they stood about their chief, and fought there and would not leave him, and the Piegans could not drive them.

Not very long after the fight began, some of the people found lying on the prairie the bodies of the old chief Many Horses and his wife, and a man named Calf Bull, shouted out: "Now fight well and do your best. Our old chief is killed. We have found him over here dead. Let us take vengeance on these enemies." The Piegans all cried out, "Our father and our chief is killed!" and they all made a noise and slapped their mouths and made a rush for the Crows.

In another part of the field one of the enemy, who could talk good Piegan, stepped out to one side and held up a pistol and said: "Piegans, here is your great chief's gun. I have killed him and taken it. Take courage now." Then an old Piegan, named Stinking Head, called out to the Piegans: "Men, women, and boys! Old men, young men, and children! They have killed our great chief! Take great courage!" Then they all took courage and shouted the warcry.

When the Piegans all learned that Many Horses had been killed, they made so fierce a charge that the enemy turned and ran. In a *coulée* toward the Cypress Hills they had built some breastworks of stones, and when the Piegans made this charge, the Crows and Gros Ventres ran to get behind this shelter. But the Piegans were so close behind them that they did not stop there, but ran on and out of the breastworks on the other side, before they stopped and turned to fight. The Piegans were close behind them, and Wolf Calf was riding ahead of all the others. There was a Crow running on foot behind the rest, and Wolf Calf dropped his rein and got ready to shoot this man. He thought the young colt he was riding was then running as fast as it could, but when he fired his gun at the Crow, the horse ran so much faster that before he could catch his rein to stop it, he was right in the midst of the Crows. Half a dozen shot at him, killing his horse and wounding him in the leg above the ankle. As it happened, none of the Crows near him now had loaded guns, but when his horse went down, they all fell upon him and began to pound him with their coup sticks and whip handles. Then the Piegans who were near called out, "Come! let us make a charge and save the old man before he gets killed!" They rushed in and drove the enemy back, and rescued Wolf Calf; White Calf, and two others, now dead, pulling him out of the *mêlée*.

Wolf Tail this day did two brave things. Some Piegans had surrounded a Gros Ventre, who was called He Stabbed a Good Many. This man still had his gun loaded, and was pointing it at the Piegans and keeping them off, for they were afraid of him. Wolf Tail was the last of the Piegans to get to him. He rode up to the Gros Ventre, jumped off his horse, snatched the gun, and took it away from him. Then he called out to the Piegans: "Come on now; there is no longer any danger. Come up and kill him!"

Wolf Tail walked away from the Gros Ventre, who was then killed by one of the Piegans.

After this he came up with another Gros Ventre, who was shooting arrows. He also had a lance. Wolf Tail rode up behind him, jumped off his horse, and seized the man. He took away from him his lance and arrows, pulled out his pistol, and shot him.

The Crows and Gros Ventres were now all running away, and the Piegans were following and killing them. They began with those who were on foot, cutting them off a few at a time, killing the men and taking the women and boys prisoners. There are now some middle-aged men in the Piegan camp who were taken in this fight.

At last the footmen were all killed, and they made a charge on the mounted men. They cut off a bunch of these from the main body, and rushed them toward a cut *coulée* and over a steep bank; but when the Piegans saw the enemy falling down the side of the *coulée,* they rode around it and caught those who mere left alive as they were coming out, and killed them in bunches of four or five. They kept following the main body for hours, and at last they had been running and fighting so long that all the Indians were now very tired, and they could no longer run, but the enemy were walking away and the Piegans walking after them. The enemy's horses would give out and stop, and the Piegans would kill the riders, for by this time the Crows and Gros Ventres were so frightened that they no longer showed fight, and the Piegans had no trouble in killing them. Some one overtook an old Gros Ventre, who called out: "Spare me! I am old!" The Piegan's heart was touched and he was going to spare him, but another man ran up and said,

"Oh, yes, we will spare you," and he blew out his brains.

Very few of the enemy were killed with guns. It was not necessary. They killed some by running over them with their horses, others with bows and arrows, others with hatchets, some they lanced, pounded some on the heads with whips, stabbed some, and killed some with stones. They followed them about eighteen miles. The trail that they made was a mile and a half wide, and all along this the enemy were dropped, here two or three, there half a dozen, as thick as buffalo after a killing.

At last they reached the gap in the Cypress Hills where the pines are, and the enemy got in among the timber. Then the Piegans said: "Come. That will do. We have killed enough. Let us stop here and go back." So they returned to their camp. They counted as they were going back more than four hundred dead of the enemy, and there must have been many more who had crawled into the grass and died.

After the fight was over and the Piegans had turned back, a Gros Ventre woman, whose husband had been killed and her daughter captured, made up her mind that she would go back and look for them. When she got into the timber, she said to the others who were with her, "My man is killed and my daughter is gone, and I am going down into the Piegan camp to find out what has become of her." She still had a horse and rode down the mountain after the Piegans. Lying on the prairie there was a Gros Ventre Indian, who had been knocked down and scalped, and had pretended that he was dead. Some time after the Piegans had gone he opened his eyes, and as he did so, he saw this woman riding by him.

He called out to her and asked her to take him back to the Gros Ventres, but she refused, telling him that she was going to look for her daughter. The man got up on his feet, but the skin of his forehead hung down over his eyes so that it blinded him, and he had to hold it up with one hand in order to see. He walked toward the woman, who had stopped, talking to her, and when he had come close to her, he made a rush toward her, so as to get hold of the horse's tail and take the horse away from the woman, so that he could ride after his people. But when he tried to grasp the tail, he reached out with both hands to catch it, and the skin dropped over his eyes and blinded him, and he stumbled and fell, and the woman avoided him, and presently when he got up and lifted his skin, the woman was a good way off. She rode on to the Piegan camp and found her daughter there, and both were adopted into the tribe and died there.

Up to the time when they returned to their own camp, the Piegans had not known how many of their own people they had lost. Now they learned that three great chiefs, six warriors, and one woman had been killed. Then all the Piegans cried, because they thought so much of their chief Many Horses. His relations spoke to Four Bears, the camp orator, and he went out through the camp and called out and said: "Let every person bring one blanket each for the burial of this chief, and each one who brings a blanket shall take a rope and catch one horse out of his band." The people did this, and gave Many Horses a great funeral, for all liked him and his wife, because they had been kind and generous to everybody.

Some time after the funeral, Four Bears went out again through the camp and shouted out: "Bring out your captives, your women and children that you have taken. Bring out all the things that you have taken— shields, guns, arrows, bows, scalps, medicine pipes; everything of value that you have taken—and put them in a pile so that we can look at them." The people did this, and it made a fine show. When all these things were spread out, some great warrior went along the line and took up each thing in turn, as he came to it, and shouted out the name of the person who had taken it, so that everybody would know who was brave. This was a *coup*. Even women and children counted *coups* on the things they had taken.

CHAPTER IX.

IMPLEMENTS AND INDUSTRIES.

THE white man found the Indian a savage in the stone age of development. For the most part the flesh of beasts and the wild fruits of the earth nourished him, skins sheltered and clad him, wood, stone, and bone armed and equipped him. He had no knowledge of metals, but he had learned how to fashion the stone mace or warclub, to chip out flint knives and arrow-points, to tan skins, to bake pots, and had invented that complex weapon the bow and arrow. He had a hunting companion, the dog, which was also his beast of burden.

No one now can tell the story of the Indian's advance in culture: what was the history of the bow or the stone-pointed arrow; who first devised the lodge or the dog travois. All these things are said to have been given them by the Creator, who had pity on his children, once without means of defence against the stronger beasts, and who starved when roots and berries were not to be had. For tradition tells us of a time between the creation of the red man and the coming of the white man, when the Indian lacked even the simple weapons that his Creator gave him later. Some of the stories say that then men had no hands, only paws, armed with long claws like a bear, and that with these they unearthed the roots of the prairie, or drew down to their faces the branches of the berry bushes laden with ripe fruit. Then, indeed, the people were poor, weak, and ignorant, and had no means of getting a living. Then they must have been a prey to the wild creatures. The buffalo are said to have eaten them, and not only the buffalo but the deer and the antelope as well. After this, the stories go on, they learned the art of making snares and traps, in which they took the smaller wild creatures, whose flesh furnished them a part of their subsistence, and whose skins were their first clothing. The club no doubt they already had, and from this the evolution of the stone-headed axe or hammer was natural. With these they pounded to death the animals that they caught in their snares. Perhaps the knife was next invented, and then the lance—which is only a knife with a long handle—and this may sometimes have been thrown from the hand. Last, and by far the greatest of all, must have come the wonderful discovery of the bow and arrow. But of the manner of these inventions and of their sequence no memory or tradition now remains.

For the most part the Indians of the West lived in skin lodges. This was partly because such dwellings were warm, dry, and easily obtained, but especially because they were light and convenient and could readily be moved about from place to place, and so were in all respects suited to the needs of a nomadic people. But not all the Indians were dwellers in tents. The evolution of the house had progressed far beyond the single-roomed shelter of grass or bark or skins. The Indians of the East had large connected houses of poles, sometimes fortified. The Pawnees and Mandans built great sod or dirt houses, in which many families lived in common, the sleeping places about the walls being separated by permanent wooden partitions, while in front of each a curtain was let down so as to form an actual room. Further to the south are still in use the many-roomed, many-storied houses of the Pueblo people, which were the highest development of the house among the Indians north of Mexico.

Tradition warrants us in believing that many tribes who now live in lodges once had permanent houses, and that the exclusive use of skin lodges among the plains tribes may have come about in comparatively recent times. Many of these tribes have lived on these plains for a short time only—say two or three centuries—having migrated thither from some earlier home, and many of them have traditions of a time when they lived in permanent houses, though often the story is so vague that nothing is known of the character of these dwellings. The Pawnees, on the other hand, say that in their ancient home—which was probably on the Pacific slope—they dwelt in houses built of stone.

The highest development of architecture within the historic period was in the south, as shown by the ruins of Central America, Mexico, and Arizona; yet tribes who lived in the north, whether on the Atlantic or Pacific slopes, had permanent dwellings, and it seems probable that those which we have known only as nomads may have retrograded in this respect, and lost the art of building which they once possessed.

The common movable home of the plains tribes was the conical tipi made of a number of dressed buffalo skins, sewed together and supported by about sixteen lodge poles. To the north, among the Lake Winnipeg Chippeways, the tipi covering is of birch bark, which, when done up for transportation, is in seven rolls. The largest and longest when unrolled reaches around the lodge poles at the ground from one side of the door to the other; the one next in length fits around the lodge poles above the lower strip, lapping a little over it, so as to shed the rain. One still shorter goes on above this, and so on to the top of the cone. At both ends of each strip there is a lath-like stick of wood to keep the bark from fraying or splitting. The pieces of which these strips are composed are neatly sewed together with tamarak roots—*wattap'*. There are no wings or ears about the smokeholes of such a lodge, but these are not needed in the timber where it is used.

The large sod houses of the Pawnees, Arickaras, and Mandans, have often been described. The Wichitas build odd-looking beehive-like dwellings of grass; the hogans of the Navajoes are of brush and sticks; both walls and roofs of the houses of the northwest coast Indians are made of shakes, split from the cedar. On the whole, the difference between the homes of the various tribes is very great.

Food supply and defence against enemies depended on the warrior's weapons. These were his most precious possessions, and he gave much care to their manufacture. Knowing nothing of metals, he made his edge tools of sharpened stones. Let us see how the arrow-maker worked.

The camp is sleepy, for it is midday and the heat of the blazing sun has driven almost every one to seek the shade. The few young men who have not gone out to hunt are asleep in the lodges, and most of the women have put aside for the time their work on the hides and meat, and are sitting in the lodges sewing moccasins, or else are pounding choke cherries, seated on the ground beneath skins spread over poles to make a shade. Only here and there one, old and very industrious, is hard at work, careless of the heat. Even the children for the time have stopped their noise and retired to the fringe of bushes along the stream, where they are playing quietly. Near a lodge, small and weather-beaten, two men seated under a shade are hard at work. Each holds between his knees a block of stone, from which, by light sharp blows of a small stone hammer, he is chipping off triangular flakes of flint for making arrowheads. The material used by one of the men is a black obsidian obtained by trade from the Crows to the south, while the other has a piece of milky chalcedony picked up in the mountains to the west. Each of these blocks has been sweated by being buried in wet earth, over which a fire has been built, the object of this treatment being to bring to light all the cracks and checks in the stone, so that no unnecessary labour need be performed on a piece too badly cracked to be profitably worked. As the workmen knock off the chips, they turn the blocks, so that after a little they become roughly cylindrical, always growing smaller and smaller, until at length each is too small to furnish more flakes. They are then put aside.

Each man now collects all the flakes he had knocked off, and, piling them together on one corner of his robe, carefully examines each one. Some are rejected at a glance, some put in a pile together as satisfactory, while over others the arrow-maker ponders for a while, as if in doubt. Presently he seems to have satisfied himself, and prepares for his second operation. For this he takes in his left palm a pad of

11

buckskin large enough to cover and protect it while holding the sharp flake, while over his right hand he slips another piece of tanned hide something like a sailmaker's "palm," and used for the same purpose. Against his "palm" the arrow-maker places the head of a small tool—a straight piece of deer or antelope horn or of bone—about four inches long, and pressing its point against the side of the piece of flint held in the other hand, he flakes off one little chip of the stone and then another close to it, thus passing along the edge of the unformed flint until one side of it is straight, and then along the other. He works quickly and apparently without much care, except when he is near the point, for this is a delicate place, and carelessness or haste here may endanger the arrowhead; for, if its point should be broken, it is good for nothing. Sometimes an unseen check will cause the head to break across without warning, and the labour expended on this particular piece is thus wasted. But usually the arrow-maker works rapidly and spoils but few points. After the head is shaped, there are often left some thin projecting edges which mar its symmetry and add nothing to its effectiveness. These are broken off either by pressure or by a sharp blow with some light instrument, such as a bit of bone or of hard wood.

The making of these stone points has now been almost entirely forgotten, but I have seen a beautiful and perfect dagger, six or eight inches long, made from a piece of glass bottle.

There is a wide variation in the shape and size of these stone points. Some are very small, others large, some are fine and delicate, and others coarse and clumsy. The edges are usually regular and fairly smooth, but sometimes serrated. A wound inflicted by one of them is said to have been much more serious than that inflicted by a hoop-iron point, and the Indian of to-day believes that the stone points had somewhat the effect of a poisoned arrowhead. There is a grain of foundation for this, since the stone point would make a ragged wound, and the point if deeply buried in the flesh could not easily be extracted or pushed on through, but would readily become detached from the arrow shaft. On the other hand, it would make a clean wound, which would heal much more easily than a bullet wound.

These arrowheads were roughly triangular in shape, but often had a short shank for attachment to the shaft. This shank, or the middle part of the short side of the triangle, was set into a notch in the shaft, fastened by a glue made from the hoofs of the buffalo, and made additionally secure by being whipped in place by fine sinew strings, put on wet.

The arrow shafts are not less important than the heads. They should be straight, strong, and heavy, and for this reason year-old shoots of the dogwood, cherry, or service berry make the best arrow wood. The Indians of the southwest use reeds of the cane, and with them the shaft is often composed of three or more pieces. Some tribes use shoots of the willow, but this warps so readily and is so light and weak that it will hardly be employed if any other wood can be had. The length and thickness of the shaft varies with the tribe —as does also the manner of feathering, of fastening on the heads, and of painting—but it almost always has two or three winding grooves throughout its length, the purpose of which is said to be to facilitate the flow of blood, and probably also the arrow's entrance into the flesh. The arrow shafts, after being cut and scraped free from bark, are bound together in bundles and hung up to dry in the lodge, where it is warm. When partly seasoned, they are taken down and picked over. Those which are not entirely straight are handled, bent this way and that, and the bundle is then again hung up, and left until the wood is thoroughly seasoned, when the shafts are again gone over and the bad ones rejected. Usually they are brought down to the proper thickness by scraping with a bit of flint or glass, or with a knife, but often a slab of grooved sandstone is used for this purpose. This has the same effect as if they were sandpapered down. The grooves in the shaft are made by passing it through a hole bored through a rib or a vertebra's dorsal spine, or sometimes, it is said, by pressure of the teeth, in which the wood is held while being bent. This hole is just large enough for the shaft to pass through, and is circular, except for one or two projections, which press into the wood and cut out the grooves. The feathers are usually three in number, put on with glue, but wound above and below with sinew. The notch for the string is deep and in the same plane with the arrow's head. The private mark of the owner is usually found close to the end of the feathers. It may be a fashion of painting or some arrangement of stained feathers. The feathers are rarely two or four, and their length varies greatly with the tribe. They are usually taken from birds of prey.

The most important part of the warrior's equipment was the bow, and over no part of it was more time and labour spent. In every lodge there were kept sticks of bow wood, some of them so far advanced in manufacture that but little labour was required to complete them. While the bow was usually made of wood, bone and horn were also used. Those of bone were fashioned of two or more pieces of the rib of some large animal—an elk or a buffalo—neatly fitted and spliced together. Those of elk horn were also made of several pieces, fitted and glued together, and wrapped with sinew. Buffalo or sheep horn bows were made of several pieces, which were boiled or steamed and straightened before being put together. Bows made of horn or bone were very stiff, and sometimes could hardly be drawn by a white man, though handled by their owners with apparent ease. Their manufacture was a long, slow process, and they were highly valued, and it was not easy to induce an owner to sell one. They were made chiefly among the mountain Indians, such as the Crows, Snakes, and Utes, but were often traded to other tribes.

Almost all the native woods in one section of the country or another were used for bows. In later times hickory was a favourite wood, and old oxbows were highly valued by the Indians, who used to steam and straighten them and then make them into bows. Other woods employed were the osage orange, ash, cedar, yew, choke cherry, and willow. The wood was seasoned with care, worked down carefully, straightened again and again, oiled and handled, and, finally, as the last operation, the nocks were cut, the sinew backing applied, a wrapping of buckskin secured about the grip of the bow, and it was finished. Good bows of plains and mountain tribes were always backed with sinew, which added much to the spring and strength of the weapon. Some tribes toward the Pacific coast backed their bows with salmon skin. The bowstring was always made of twisted sinew.

The bow and arrows were carried in a bow case and quiver, fastened together and slung over the shoulder. The covering of these was often otter or panther skin, the hide of a buffalo calf, or, in later times, of domestic cattle.

Among most of the plains tribes the use of the bow was discontinued long ago, and at the present time only boys' bows are in use. The old familiarity and skill with the arm are lost. In old times, however, the bow at short range was an extremely effective weapon, and a skilled archer could shoot so rapidly that he had no difficulty in keeping several horizontally directed arrows in the air at the same time. The bow could be shot more rapidly and effectively than a revolving pistol.

The power of the bow is well known. There are perfectly well authenticated instances where two buffalo, running side by side, have been killed by the same arrow, and it was not uncommon for an arrow to go so far through an animal that the point and a part of the shaft projected on the other side. The arrow could be shot to a distance of three or four hundred yards.

The stone axe, the maul, and the lance were all simple weapons. The axehead was usually of soft stone, ground down to an edge, and a groove was worked out at right angles to its length, so that the green withe by which it was fastened to the handle should not slip off. Over this, green rawhide was sewed with sinew, and this hide usually extended over the whole length of the handle. The maul or war-club was made of a grooved oval stone, fastened to a handle in the same way as the axe. The club had a long handle and carried a small stone, no larger than a man's fist. The woman's maul was short handled and the stone was large and heavy. The lancehead was made of flint, flaked sharp, and lashed to a shaft with sinew or wet rawhide strings.

A very important part of the warrior's outfit was the shield, with which he stopped or turned aside the arrows of his enemy. It was usually circular in shape, and was made of the thick, shrunken hide of a buffalo bull's neck. It was heavy enough to turn the ball from an old-fashioned smooth-bored gun. The shield was usually highly ornamented, and often had the warrior's "medicine" painted on it, and was often fringed with eagle feathers about its circumference.

Clothing was made of skins tanned with or without the fur. Buffalo tribes, as a rule, wore clothing made for the most part of the skins of this animal, and used comparatively little buckskin. As their work was chiefly on these large heavy skins, they were poor tanners by comparison with those tribes which lived in the mountains and made their clothing largely of deer skin. The leggings, shirts, and women's dresses, have often been described. Moccasins for summer wear covered the foot only, not coming up over the ankle, but winter moccasins were provided with a high flap which tied about the ankle under the legging. Some tribes used moccasins made wholly of deer skin and without a sole; with others a parfleche sole was always provided. They were ornamented in front with stained porcupine quills, or in later times with beads; sometimes, too, there are little fringes about the ankle or down the front, and two little tags from the heels. All the sewing of this clothing was done with thread made of sinew, and in old times with awls made of bone or stiff thorns. Such sewing was very enduring, and the dressed skin would wear out before the seams gave way.

Many of the tribes—especially those to the south—made a simple pottery, either formed on a mould or else within or without a frame of basket-work, which sometimes was afterward burned away in the baking. The best pottery, that of the southwest, was often, if not always, made by coiling a long rope of clay, tier above tier, until the vessel was completed. Some of the ware so made was singularly graceful and perfect. Often it was ornamented by indented markings drawn while the clay was soft, or by figures painted before the baking. With the advent of the whites and the introduction of vessels of metal, the manufacture of such pottery ceased, and it is now carried on in but very few tribes.

Among the northern tribes, where pottery was least known, ladles, spoons, bowls, and dishes were usually formed from horn or wood. The horns of the buffalo, the mountain sheep, and the white goat were used for these purposes, those of the last-named species being often elaborately carved and ornamented by the north-west coast tribes. Plates or dishes made of pieces of buffalo horn fitted and sewn together with sinew were common. Excrescences on tree trunks, knocked off and hollowed out, made good wooden bowls. Stone pots and ollas and stone mortars were common, especially on the southwest coast, as were also the basalt mills used for grinding the corn, metates. Some plains tribes used wooden mortars, usually made of oak or some other hard wood, with a long and heavy wooden pestle. The Lake Winnipeg Chippeways still use a mill of two circular stones, revolving one upon the other, but the idea of this may have been borrowed from the whites. By some tribes cups and buckets were made from the lining of the buffalo's paunch, and many others wove basketware, so tight that it would hold water, and such vessels were even used to cook in, the water being heated with hot stones.

Implements for tanning—fleshers—were made of stone, with the edges flaked off until they were sharp, or of elkhorn steamed and bent at one end for three inches at right angles to the course of the antler and sharpened, or of bone, as the cannon bone of a buffalo, cut diagonally so as to give a sharp edge, and notched along this sharpened border. All these were serviceable, and were commonly employed.

The different tribes had but slight knowledge of the textile art, and this knowledge seems to have been greatest in the south and on the coast. Many tribes wove baskets and mats of reeds and grass, yet the plains Indians, who had in the fleece of the buffalo an excellent material for weaving cloth, never seem to have got any further than to twist ropes from it. The Mokis of the south and the coast tribes of the north practised the aboriginal art of blanket-weaving, and the Navajoes, after they obtained their flocks from the Spaniards, took up this art and now practise it in singular perfection. The blanket-weaving of the north is less skilful. The rounded hats woven of cedar bark by the northwest coast tribes deserve mention. The plains tribes plaited ropes of rawhide; those of the northern coast make ropes of cedar bark, and long fishing-lines by knotting together the slender stems of the kelp.

Three vehicles were known to the primitive In-

dian—the travois in the south and the sledge in the
north for land travel, and the canoe wherever there
were water ways. The sledge could be used only when
the ground was snow-covered, and it was scarcely
known south of the parallel of 50°. In primitive
times both sledge and travois were drawn by dogs, but
as soon as horses were obtained, the dogs were freed
from the travois, and horses drew the loads. From
time immemorial the travois has been used by the
plains savage to transport his possessions, and it is
only when he makes his first slow step toward civilization that he exchanges it for a wagon. What his
canoe is to the Indian who traverses the water ways of
the north, or his dog sledge to the fur-clad Innuit, the
travois* is to the dweller on the plains. Where in
use to-day, it consists of two poles about the size of
lodge poles, crossed near their smaller ends, and toward
the larger held in place by crosspieces three feet apart.
The space between these two cross braces is occupied
by a stiff rawhide netting running from one pole to
the other, and strong enough to carry a weight of several hundred pounds. The crossed ends of the poles
are placed over a horse's withers just at the front of
the saddle, and the separated braced ends drag upon
the ground behind. The body and hips of the horse
are in the empty space between the angles at the
withers and the first crosspiece, which comes close
behind the hocks. Bearing a part of the weight on
his shoulders, the horse drags this rude contrivance

---

*This is a French trapper word, perhaps a corruption of
travers or *à travers,* across, referring to the crossing of the
poles over the horse's withers. It hardly seems that it can come
from *travaux* or *traineau,* as has been suggested.

Piegan Travois

and its load over the rough prairie, along narrow mountain trails or through hurrying torrents, with rarely a mishap. On the platform of the travois are carried loads of meat from the buffalo-killing, the various possessions of the owner in moving camp from place to place, a sick or wounded individual too weak to ride, and sometimes a wickerwork cage shaped like a sweat lodge, in which are confined small children, or even a family of tiny puppies with their mother. Things that cannot be conveniently packed on the backs of the horses are put upon the travois. Sometimes the travois bears the dead, for with certain tribes it is essential to the future well-being of the departed that they be brought back to the tribal burying ground near the village.

The highest type of Indian canoe is that of birch bark, employed by the tribes of the north and northeast, yet in many respects the canoe of the northwest coast equals or excels it. The latter being of wood, and of one piece, is much more substantial than the birch; yet even it must be cared for, since a rough knock or two on the beach may split it from end to end, and if it should receive injury, the work of repairing is much more difficult than that of patching a bark canoe. The vessels used on the northwestern coast vary in length from ten to eighty feet, and are hollowed out from the trunk of a single tree of the white cedar. After the tree trunk has been flattened above and roughly shaped, the work of hollowing it out begins. Fires are built on the top of the log, carefully watched, and so controlled that they burn evenly and slowly down into the wood. When they have gone far enough, they are extinguished, the interior is scraped, and then the canoe-builder, using a wooden handle in which is fastened a small chisel, carefully goes over the whole surface. At each blow he takes off a little scale of wood, as large as a man's thumb and quite thin, and this he continues, within and without, until the canoe is completed. It is then braced by two or more crosspieces, which are sewed to the gunwales with steamed cedar twigs on either side, so that the vessel cannot spread. The painting follows, and the vessel is ready for use. Only seasoned and perfect timber is used for these canoes.

In such canoes, the Indians of the north Pacific make long journeys over the open seas, often venturing out of sight of land, facing rough weather, and capturing sea otters, seals, sea lions, and whales. The larger canoes were used to carry war parties, and the sudden appearance of one of these great boats full of fighting men carried consternation to the hearts of the dwellers in the village that it threatened. Travellers in these canoes, when they meet a heavy head wind, are often obliged to lie windbound for days before they can continue their journey.

Besides the long pointed paddles with a crossbar at the handle, which are used to propel the canoes, each of the larger ones is provided with a mast stepped in a chock in the bottom, and supported by one of the forward crossbars. A spritsail is used with a following wind, but as the canoes have no keel, it is impossible to beat, and even with a beam wind the vessel slips rapidly off to leeward.

Dugouts widely different from those of the northwest coast, and canoes made of pine or spruce bark, are used by some of the canoe people of the northern Rocky Mountains, the Kutenais, Kalispels, and others. Those of bark arc quite remarkable in type, being much longer on the bottom than the top, and terminating before and behind in a long slender point, which looks somewhat like the ram of a man-of-war. The bark is stripped off the tree trunk in a single piece, the outer surface being shaved or scraped smooth. It is then bent inside out, so that the inside of the canoe is formed of the outside of the bark. The ends are then brought together and sewed up with long fibres of roots, the awl or needle used being of bone. The seams are pitched with gum from the spruce. The gunwale on either side is strengthened by strips of hard wood, sewn to the bark by roots or cedar bark, and these strips meet and are fastened together at either end of the boat, and along the cut edge of the bark on either side of the two ends, a strip of hard wood is sewn and the two strips lashed together. The boat is strengthened by ribs of hard wood, which run across from one gunwale to the other, following the skin of the canoe, and a number of longitudinal strips form a flooring and strengthen the sides. Thus the vessel, like the birch canoe, has a real frame, though this is built inside the skin, reversing the usual order. Crossbars or thwarts run from gunwale to gunwale, and give additional stiffness. Sometimes the bark immediately below the gunwales is from the birch tree. The paddle has a straight, simple handle, without crosspiece. These canoes are thus quite elaborate, but they are extremely difficult to handle by one who is not accustomed to them, and turn over on very small provocation.

The birch bark canoe of the northern Indians is identical with that used in the east, and its form and material are familiar to all. It is a graceful, seaworthy structure, very light and easily transported from place to place, and very readily repaired. It is in general use throughout the north.

On the plains, canoes are unknown, for there are no water ways which make them necessary, and though many tribes which had migrated from the east had in their earlier homes made and used these vehicles, yet when the conditions of their life made them unnecessary, the art of building them was soon forgotten. On some of the larger streams, however, boats were needed to ferry across the chattels of the people when travelling, and this want was supplied by the invention of the "bull boat." This was something like the skin coracle of the ancient Britons, but was even more primitive. It was a circular vessel, shaped like a shallow teacup, made of a fresh buffalo hide stretched over a frame of green willow branches. All the holes in the skin were sewed up, and all the seams pitched with tallow. The vessel was carefully loaded with goods for transportation, a place being left at one point for the paddler. Owing to the shape of the boat, it could not be rowed or paddled in the ordinary way. The woman dipped her paddle in the water and drew it directly toward her, and toward the side of the boat, and in this way pulled the boat to the opposite shore. Men did not often use these boats, but usually swam over with the horses. Such boats were not permanent, for as soon as they had served their purpose, the frames were torn out of them and the hides were used for some other purpose. Bull boats were used chiefly on the lower Missouri and Platte rivers. On the upper Missouri, rafts were the only means of ferrying across the streams.

The Indian's ideas of art are rude. He has an eye for bright colors, but no notion of drawing. His figures of men and animals are grotesque, and are as grotesquely painted in staring hues of red, yellow, and black, his paints being burned clays and charcoal. In his pottery and his carving, however, he is more advanced. Some of his mater jars and other vessels have very graceful shapes, and some pots, representing human heads, which have been exhumed from the ancient mounds, are full of character.

It is in the art of carving, however, that the greatest skill was shown. Using the soft catlinite of the pipe-stone quarry, the plains warrior whittled out his great red pipe as symmetrically as if turned in a lathe, often ornamenting it with the head and neck of a horse or a bear. The canoe man of Puget Sound carved the soft cedar of the canoe prow into a figure-head. The Navajoes of the south and the Haidahs of the north are skilled silversmiths to-day, and the dwellers on the British Columbia and Alaskan coasts still fashion the great totem poles, which tell the story of their descent from some mythical ancestor. Very remarkable skill is shown by the Queen Charlotte's Sound Indians in their work in a black slate rock which they carve into all sorts of shapes. I have seen platters and dishes, pipes, and models of houses, beautifully carved and often inlaid with carved bits of ivory taken from the teeth of the walrus or the whale.

Great time and patience must be expended on this work, and on the drilling of straight holes through the stems of their pipes, some of them four feet in length. While the bowls of these pipes are most often of the stone known as catlinite, sometimes they are of wood or bone, or even petrified wood or quartz pebble.

The musical instruments of the Indians are few. Drums, whistles, rattles, an instrument called by the whites a "fiddle"—consisting of a gourd and notched stick along which another stick is drawn—and a flageolet with three or four stops were the principal ones. The flageolet used by some tribes is an instrument of considerable range and power, and the music made on it, heard at night in the camp when some young man is serenading his sweetheart, is very charming. The whistles are used chiefly in war, the drums in festal or religious ceremonies, the rattles to beat time at the dance or to frighten away bad spirits. This rattle is one of the important possessions of the healer, and is often so highly valued that the owner refuses to sell it.

The music of these people is chiefly vocal. They are unwearied singers, and love, war, religion, sorrow, or joy are alike expressed in their songs.

Quatsena Village, West Coast Vancouver Island

CHAPTER X.

MAN AND NATURE.

LIKE the wild bird and the beast, like the cloud and the forest tree, the primitive savage is a part of nature. He is in it and of it. He studies it all through his life. He can read its language. It is the one thing that he knows. He is an observer. Nothing escapes his eye. The signs of clouds, the blowing of the winds, the movements of birds and animals—all tell to him some story. It is by observing these signs, reading them, and acting on them that he procures his food, that he saves himself from his enemies, that he lives his life.

But though a keen observer, the Indian is not a reasoner. He is quick to notice the connection between two events, but often he does not know what that connection is. He constantly mistakes effect for cause, *post hoc* for *propter hoc*. If the wind blows and the waves begin to roll on the surface of the lake, he says that the rolling of the waves causes the blowing of the breeze. The natural phenomena which we understand so little, he does not understand at all. In his attempts to assign causes for them, he gives explanations which are grotesque. The moon wanes because it is sick, and at last it dies and a new one is created; or it grows small because mice are gnawing at its edges, nibbling it away. He hears a grouse

rise from the ground with a roar of wings, and con-
cludes that the roar of the thunder must be made by
a bird much larger; or he sees an unknown bird rise
from the ground, and just as it flies the thunder rolls,
hence this bird causes the thunder and is the thunder
bird.

To him the sun, moon, and stars are persons.
The animals, trees, and mountains are powers and in-
telligences. The ravens foretell events to come, the
wolves talk to him of matters which are happening at
a distance. If he is unhappy and prays fervently for
help, some animal may take pity on him and assist
him by its miraculous power. He understands his
own weakness and realizes the strength of the forces
of nature. He realizes, too, their incomprehensibility.
To him they are mysteries.

The Indian's life is full of things that he does not
understand—of the mysterious, of the superhuman.
These mysteries he greatly fears, and he prays without
ceasing that he may be delivered from the unknown
perils which threaten him on every hand. He has a
wholesome dread of material dangers, of enemies on
the warpath, of bears in the mountains; but far more
than these he fears the mysterious powers that sur-
round him—powers which are unseen until they strike,
which leave no tracks upon the ground, the smoke of
whose fires cannot be seen rising through the clear air.
He fears the burning arrow shot by the thunder; the
unseen under-water animals which may seize him, as
he is crossing stream or lake, and drag him beneath
the waves; the invisible darts of evil spirits which
cause disease not to be cured by any medicine of roots
or herbs; the ghost, terrible not for what it may do,
but only because it is a ghost. Against such dangers

he feels that he has no defence. So it is that he prays to the sun, the moon, the stars, the mountains, the ghosts, the above-people, and the under-water people. For pity and for protection he appeals to everything in nature that his imagination indues with a power greater than his own.

In an Indian camp it is not the average man that has communication with the other and unseen world. All pray, it is true, but to most of these prayers no answer is vouchsafed. It is only now and then that visions or communications from the supernatural world come to men and women. Those who are thus especially favoured are not, so far as we can tell from their histories, particularly deserving. The help that they receive they owe not so much to any good works that they have performed, or to any merit of their own, as to the kindness of heart of the supernatural powers. In another volume* I have given some account of the practice of dreaming for power, an act of penance and self-sacrifice which, when carried out, often secured the pity and help of the supernatural powers, and which seems to have been well-nigh universal among the Indians.

The powers influencing the Indian's life may be either malignant or beneficent, but by far the greater number seem to be well disposed and helpful. Stories about this latter class are much more numerous than those of hurtful powers, and it seems that usually these supernatual beings are easily moved by prayer and accessible to pity. On the other hand, a man who fails to show respect to these forces is likely to die. On the west side of the Rocky Mountains, there is a

---

*Blackfoot Lodge Tales, p. 191.

mountain sheep skull grown into a great pine tree trunk. This is a sacred object, reverenced by all. Once, however, a Nez Percé laughed at his companions because they offered presents to this skull, and to show that he did not believe in it he shot at it with his gun. The next day as he was travelling along his rifle, accidentally discharged, killed him.

The depths of the water shelter a horde of mysterious inhabitants. Some of them are people, but quite different from those who live on the prairie. Others are animals similar to those which we have on land, while others are monsters. The under-water people use the water fowl—the swans, geese, and pelicans—for their dogs; that is, for their beasts of burden. Small water birds are used as messengers by the supernatural powers. The Dakotas and Cheyennes tell us that the under-water monsters have long horns and are covered with hair. The Cheyennes say that they lay eggs, and that any human being who eats one of these eggs, shortly becomes himself one of these water monsters.

With some prairie tribes there seems in early times to have been a tendency to explain the advent of any animal new to them by concluding that it was an under-water animal that had taken to living on the land. Thus, by some, the first white men were thought to be under-water people, just as by others they were believed to be spirits or mysteries. The Piegans tell with much detail how the first horses came up out of a lake. The story which was first told me by Almost-a-Dog, and since by other old people, is this:

A long time ago a Piegan warrior's dream told him about a lake far away, where there were some large animals, which were harmless and which he could catch, tame, and use to pack on, like dogs. And because they were very large and could carry a heavy load, they would be better to use than the dogs, on which the people then carried their packs. "Go to this lake," said his dream, "and take with you a rope, so that you can catch these animals."

So the man took a long rope of bull's hide, and went to the shore of the lake, and dug a hole in the sand there, and hid in it. While he watched, he saw many animals come down to the lake to drink. Deer came down and coyotes and elk and buffalo. They all came and drank. After a while, the wind began to blow and the waves to rise and roll upon the beach, saying *sh-h-h-h, sh-h-h-h.* At last came a band of large animals, unlike any that the man had ever seen before. They were big like an elk, and had small ears and long tails hanging down. Some were white, and some black, and some red and spotted. The young ones were smaller. When they came down to the water's edge and stopped to drink, his dream said to the man, "Throw your rope and catch one." So the man threw his rope, and caught one of the largest of the animals. It struggled and pulled and dragged the man about, and he was not strong enough to hold it, and at length it pulled the rope out of his hand, and the whole band ran into the lake and under the water and were not seen again. The man went back to camp feeling very sad.

He prayed for help to his dream, which said: "Four times you may try to catch these animals. If in four times trying you do not get them, you will never see them again." Then the man made a sacrifice, and prayed to the Sun and to Old Man, and his dream spoke to him in his sleep, and told him that he was not strong enough to catch a big one, that he ought try to catch one of the young—then he could hold it. The man went again to the shores of the big lake, and again dug a hole in the sand and lay hidden there. He saw all the animals come down to drink— the deer, the wolves, the elk, and the buffalo. At last the wind began to rise and the waves to roll and to say *sh-h-h-h, sh-h-h-h* upon the shore. Then came the band of strange animals to drink at the lake. Again the man threw his rope, and this time he caught one of the young and was able to hold it. He caught all of the young ones out of the band and took them to the camp. After they had been there a little while, the mares—the mothers of these colts—came trotting into the camp; their udders were full of milk. After them came all the others of the band.

At first the people were afraid of these new animals and would not go near them, but the man who had caught them told everybody that they were harmless. After a time they became tame, so that they did not have to he tied up, but followed the camp about as it moved from place to place. Then the people began to put packs on them, and they called them *po-no-kah'mi-ta,* that is, elk-dog, because they are big and shaped like an elk, and carry a pack like a dog. This is how the Piku'ni got their horses.

If the under-world is peopled with mysterious and terrible inhabitants, not less strange and powerful are those who dwell in the regions of the upper air. There lives the thunder, that fearful one, who strikes without warning, whose bolt shatters the lofty crag, blasts the tallest pine, and fells the strongest animal, a moment before active and full of life. There are the winds, the clouds, the ghosts, and many other persons, whom sometimes we feel, but never see.

As has been said, the thunder is usually regarded as a great bird, but this appears to have relation merely to the sound that it produces. Often the thunder is described as a person, sometimes as a dreadful man with threatening eyes, or again, young and handsome. Sometimes it is a monster, birdlike only in that it has wings and the power of flight. Thunder is terrible and must be prayed to, and besides this, he brings the rain which makes the crops to grow and the berries large and sweet, and for this reason, too, he must be prayed to. The rainstorm and the thunder are scarcely separated in the Indian's mind. Sometimes, when the thunder appears most dangerous, it can be frightened away. A friend of mine was once on the prairie in a very severe storm. The hair of his head and the mane of his horse stood straight out. The thunder was crashing all about him and kept drawing nearer and nearer. The man was very much frightened and did not know what to do, but at length in despair he began to shoot his gun at the thunder, loading as fast as he could, and firing in the direction of the sound. Soon after he began to do this, the thunder commenced to move away and at last ceased altogether.

Some tribes believe that a bitter hostility exists between the thunder birds and the under-water monsters, the birds attacking these last when they see them, and striving to carry them off.

The Rev. J. O. Dorsey tells of a Winnebago Indian, who was said to have been an eye witness of such a conflict, and who was called on by each of the combatants for assistance in the fight, each promising to reward him for his aid. The man was naturally very much afraid, and was doubtful what part he should take in the combat, but at length he determined to assist the thunder bird and shot an arrow into the water monster. This terminated the fight in favour of the aërial power, which then flew away with its foe. But the wounded under-water monster called back to the man, "Yes, it is true that you may become great, but your relations must die." And it was so. The man did become great, but his relations died. Sometimes, however, arrows shot by man will not injure an under-water animal. It pays no attention to the arrows.

One view taken of the thunder is given in a story told in the Blackfoot Lodge Tales; another is found in the story of the Thunder Pipe, a Blood story:

This happened long ago. In the camp the children playing, had little lodges and sticks for lodge poles, and used to make travois for their dogs. A number of them would get together and harness their dogs and move camp about a mile, carrying their little brothers and sisters, and then put up their lodges. Such was the children's play.

One day, while they were out doing this, a big cloud came up. The children said, "We had better go home. It looks as if it were going to rain." They waited too long, and before they had started, the storm began. Some went on home in the rain, and some went into the brush, to wait there till the storm had passed. It was thundering and lightening—a very hard storm. It grew worse and worse, and the thunder came closer, and those who had stayed became frightened, and at length ran home in the rain.

After the children had all reached the camp, one

was still missing—a girl about fifteen years old, very pretty. When the storm had passed, some of the people went out to look for this child, but they could not find her. This alarmed the camp, and everybody turned out to try to find the little girl. They looked for her for three days, but could not find her. The mother was very sorry to have lost her child, and gashed her legs and arms and cut off the ends of her fingers, and the father did the same. They sat up on the hills mourning, and would not eat, nor drink, nor come to camp, they were so sorry for the loss of the girl. At last the camp moved and went to another stream.

Soon after they got there, another terrible storm came up. The clouds were black, the rain poured down, and the thunder crashed everywhere about the camp. During the storm, while it was raining heaviest, a young man came running into the lodge of the mourners and said to them, "Your girl has come back." The girl was brought into the lodge, and her father and mother were very happy to see her. Before they had time to speak, she said to them, "Father and mother, I have been away, but it was not my fault." They asked her, "Where have you been?" She replied: "I cannot tell you that. I do not know where I have been. While it was raining and thundering the other day a young man came and stood beside me and said, 'Let us go.' I did not want to go, but he took me. I have been crying all the time ever since, and at last he took pity on me and brought me back. If you will go to my grandmother's lodge you will see him. He is in there. You will also find a pipestem, which your son-in-law has given me. Bring it to this lodge."

The parents went over to the lodge to get the pipe-stem, and were much surprised to see what a handsome young man was there. They did not know him. He was a stranger to them. He was so handsome they were frightened.

The old people took the stem and brought it to their lodge, and said to their daughter: "Well, it is good that you are married. Your husband is a very fine-looking man. Who is he?" She answered, "I cannot tell you, for I do not know." "When did you first see him? Where did he find you?" they said. The girl replied: "I was bending down over a tree trunk when the thunder fell right in front of me. When I raised myself up quickly and looked, this young man was standing by me. I did not wish to go with him, but he took me. We had only walked a little way when I found I was in a strange land, and I have been crying ever since. At last he said to me, 'Well, if you are so lonesome, I will have to take you back to your people.' It was a fine, bright day when we started this morning, but we had gone only a little way when we were walking in a small mist. As we came further this mist grew larger and rose and clouded over the whole sky, and we walked on in it. After a while, I found the rain pouring down, and the next thing I knew I was standing here in your camp."

The parents talked to the young man, but he would not answer them. The girl told the people that while in the strange land the young man gave her a pipe-stem to give to her father. When he was in trouble and wanted help, he might ask for it from this pipe-stem. Then the Thunder power would aid him. "When your father is tired of it," he said "he may give it to his children, and they may use it with the same power. So long as this stem is kept by your people it will be a great help to them."

This is where the stem came from that belongs to Mahkwe'yi pis'to-ki. It has been kept in this tribe, handed down from those days, and is still in the Blood camp.

The winter storms of snow and cold are ruled by a person sometimes called Coldmaker. He is white, not as the white man is white, but rather like the snow, and is clad in white, and rides a white horse. He brings the storm, riding in the midst of it, and some people have the power to call him and to bring on a snowstorm.

The wind does not often take material shape and is seldom seen, yet in some cases it speaks to people. Also it is sometimes made a messenger by the ruler. Various causes are assigned for the blowing of the wind, and one of these—told me years ago by an old Blood Indian, who knew the men to whom this happened—is perhaps worth repeating:

A good many years ago the camp was moving from the north down through this country (that along Milk River and the head waters of the Marias). When they had got down here they ran out of *l'herbe* and moved up toward the mountains to gather some, and there they saw Windmaker.

There were three young men who went out to gather *l'herbe*. They went up on the foothills, and as they were going along they saw, down below them in a valley, a strange animal. It was small—the size of a white man's cow, blue-roan in colour, and had a very long tail. They stood looking down at it, and said to each other, "What kind of an animal is that?" None of them had ever seen anything like it.

At length, while it was walking about grazing, it raised its head and looked toward them, and they saw that it had very long ears. When it looked toward them, it moved its ears backward and forward two or three times, and at once there came two or three terrible gusts of wind. It turned, and started to trot off toward the mountains, and they followed it. It threw its ears backward and forward, and gusts of wind kept coming. They chased it, and it ran into a piece of timber, in which there was a lake. Here the men separated, one going around the timber on either side of the lake, while the third followed the animal.

When the two men had gone around the timber and came to the further edge of the lake, the wind died down very suddenly. They stood there, waiting and looking for the animal. The man who had followed it saw the tracks going into the lake, and signed to the others to come to him. They, too, saw where it had gone into the water, but although they went all around the lake, they could not see any tracks where it had come out. They waited about till dark, but it did not come out of the lake, so they went back to their camp and told the medicine man what they had seen.

Before that the people had never known what it was that made the wind blow, but now, when they had seen this animal, the medicine man decided that it caused the wind, and they called it Windmaker.

The beliefs in animals are as numerous as the tribes—almost as the individuals of the tribes. Many of them have already been alluded to, or will be spoken of in the chapter on religion. The Dakotas believe that the bear and the wolf exert evil influences, and cause disease and death, while the Pawnees regard them as friendly and helpful. Besides the reverence felt for the buffalo, there are believed to exist certain mysterious buffalo which cannot be killed and which have great power.

The Pawnee Indians have a special belief about a little animal which they call ground dog, and which, from their description, I believe to be the black-footed ferret (*Putorius nigripes*). This animal, being nocturnal in habit and, spending most of its time in burrows under ground, is seldom seen. The Pawnees believe that if this animal sits up and looks at a man, working its jaws, as if chewing, the entrails of that man will at once be cut to pieces and he will die.

A considerable proportion of the "medicine" performances in any camp have to do with healing. While the Indians are skilful in curing simple ailments and in surgery of a certain kind, there are many more serious diseases which they do not at all comprehend, and for which they have no medical treatment. Such diseases they believe to be caused by evil spirits, which must be driven away by the dream power of the doctor, who relies for help on this power and not on any curative agents. The treatment consists of burning sweet-smelling vegetation to purify the air, of singing and praying to invoke the help of the power, of rattling and making alarming sounds to frighten away the evil spirits, and of sucking and brushing off the skin of the patient to remove the mechanical causes of the disease. The different operations of this healing process have often been described. Usually such treatment gives no relief and the patient dies, but in wounds or other in-juries these doctors have a success which oftentimes is very remarkable. In another place I have given some examples of this success, and I add here two other cases where men have cured themselves or were cured by others through dream power. Some of these stories come from eyewitnesses.

A small party of Piegans were camped at Fort Brule, at the mouth of the Marias River, when, one morning about daylight, a war party of enemies rushed upon them. The gates of the fort were barred, so some of the women put up their travois against the stockade and climbed over the walls for shelter, while some dug pits in the ground outside the stockade. A very heavy fight began. Two women and one man were killed just outside the stockade door by a lance in the hands of a Cree.

There was another camp of Piegans not far off, and when the fight began one of the Indians ran from Fort Brule and told these others that the Crees were attacking them. A party of warriors hur-ried down, and when they reached the fort, the Crees began to retreat. The Piegans followed them, and the two parties took their stand on a ridge, the Crees on one side and the Piegans on the other. A Piegan named White Bear was trying to get closer to the enemy, and a Cree crept up close to him and shot him through the body, the ball entering at the kid-neys and coming out at the shoulders. His compan-ions dragged the man to the camp. He was still breathing when they got him to the camp. Soon after he died.

There was an old woman in the camp, a very power-ful doctor, and when she saw that the man was dead,

Cree Lodge and Red River Cart

she took her buffalo robe and painted it on the head and on the back and down the sides. She covered the boy with the painted robe, and then asked for a dish of yellow clay and some water. When these were brought to her, she untied from White Bear's neck the skin of a little mole that he used to carry about, and put this skin in the dish of yellow clay. Then she began to sing her medicine song, and went up to the dead man and caught him by the little finger and shook him, and said, "Wake up." At this time the lodge was crowded full, and many stood about looking under the lodge skins, which were raised. The woman would shake the robe which lay on the man, and say, "Wake up; you are wanted to smoke." After she had done this four times, the fourth time she did it, this man moved. When he moved, the old woman asked that the pipe be lighted. This was done and the pipe handed to her, and after taking a small smoke and making a prayer to the ghosts, she said to the young man, "Wake up," and at the same time pulled the robe off him. White Bear staggered to his feet and reached out his hand to take the pipe, but the old woman kept backing away from him, till she came to where stood the dish of yellow chalk with the skin in it. There the man took the pipe and began to smoke, and the blood poured from both the bullet holes. He sat down beside the dish that had the mole in it, and finally lay down and smoked, and when he smoked he blew the smoke toward the mole and the yellow clay. When he had finished smoking he covered the mole-skin over with a piece of buckskin, and then after a minute or two took the skin off, and the mole was there alive, scratching and digging in the yellow clay. He lay down beside it, and the mole left the dish, ran over

on to his body, went to the bullet hole, put his head
in it, and began to pull out clots of blood. After it
had done this at one hole, it ran to the other and did
the same thing, and when it had done that, it went
back to the dish and remained there, and White Bear
again covered it with the piece of buckskin. Then
he took it off, and when he did so, there was nothing
there but the stuffed skin. After he had sung a song,
White Bear made a speech, saying that he had been
dead, but now he had come to life, and that after four
nights he would be well. The fourth day he was able
to go about.

A few days after he was able to get about, White
Bear started out as leader of a war party against the
Pend d'Oreilles. One day, as they were marching
along, he said to his fellows, "I am going ahead to
see what I can discover." A war party of the enemy saw him coming, and lay in ambush for him
in a ravine. As he was walking along with folded
arms, they fired on him, and a ball went through his
wrist and through his body. His party were not far
behind, and when they heard the shooting, they rushed
up and drove off the enemy and saved their leader.
When the fight was over White Bear said: "I am
badly hurt. We will have to go back."

They started back, and when they reached the
camp White Bear was nearly dead. They thought
he was going to die. The same doctoring was gone
through with that had been performed a few days
before, and with the same result. White Bear was
cured.

Here is another example:

The Big Snake—a Piegan—went to war. They
passed along through the Cut Bank country to go

across the mountains, and took the Good Hole through the Mountains (Cadotte) pass. One day, as they were going along, they met a war party of Crows. The Crows saw them first, and lay in ambush for them. As they were walking along, a volley was fired on them, and the leader was shot down and killed. Another one of the party was wounded, but the Piegans rushed on the Crows and drove them off.

The Piegans started back, and when they had reached the Muddy, the wounded man was nearly dead. This man had with him the stuffed skin of a curlew.

When he found that he could go no further, he stopped and asked his companions to sing his medicine song, saying that he would try whether he could do anything for himself. A sack of red paint was got out and untied, and he put the curlew skin down on the paint. The pipe was filled and handed to him lighted, and when he smoked he blew the smoke down onto the curlew skin. After the second song was sung, the curlew got up and shook itself, and dusted itself in the red paint. The man lay down on a robe spread out for him, and the curlew left the paint and walked up to him. It put its bill down in the wound and worked it about, doing this several times. Then the man turned over on his back, and the bird did the same thing to the other wound, every now and then uttering its call. After it had done this, it walked over to the red paint and sat down in it, and they covered it over with a skin. When they took the skin off, the bird was gone, and there was only the bird's skin there. The man got well at once. White Calf saw this himself.

Other stories are told in which the skin of a weasel

13

and a skunk became alive and worked similar cures, and the list might be indefinitely prolonged.

If a white man saw such things as these happen he could not explain them, and would be likely to consider them the work of the devil, or at least of some supernatural power. The Indians cannot explain them either; and believing the evidence of their eyes, they also believe that these things are done by the dream, or the secret helper, of the person who exercises the power.

All these things which we speak of as medicine the Indian calls mysterious, and when he calls them mysterious this only means that they are beyond his power to account for, that they are inexplicable. We say that the Indian calls whisky "medicine water." He really calls it mysterious water—that is, water which acts in a way that he can not understand, making him dizzy, happy, drunk. In the same way some tribes call the horse "medicine dog," and the gun "medicine iron," meaning mysterious dog and mysterious iron. He whom we call a medicine man may be a doctor, a healer of diseases; or if he is a juggler, a worker of magic, he is a mystery man. All Indian languages have words which are the equivalents of our word medicine, something with curative properties; but the Indian's translation of "medicine," used in the sense of magical or supernatural, would be mysterious, inexplicable, unaccountable.

The word "medicine," as we use it in this connection, is from the French word for doctor. The early trappers saw the possessors of this supernatural power use it in healing, and called the man who employed it a *médecin* or doctor. From calling the doctor *médecin,* it was an easy transition to call his power by the same name, and the similarity in sound of the English and French words made the term readily adopted by English-speaking people. The term "medicine man" originally meant doctor or healer, but one who effected his cures by supernatural power. So at last "medicine" came to mean this power, and "medicine man" the person who controlled the power, and the notion of curing or healing became in a measure lost.

CHAPTER XI.

HIS CREATION.

CIVILIZED man has devoted much time to specu-
lation and theory as to the origin of the Indian without as yet reaching any definite conclusion. The red
man has been assigned to different races, and has been
called a Hebrew, a Malay, and a Chinaman. Whence
he came we do not know, but it is certain that he has
inhabited this continent for a very long time—long
enough to have established here a well-differentiated
race, about whose purity and antiquity there is no
question. The curious resemblances to other races
which have so often been noticed are probably entirely fortuitous.

But if the white man gropes in darkness searching
for light as to this origin, the Indian himself has no
such doubts. Each tribe has a definite story of its
own creation, which has been handed down by oral
tradition from father to son for many generations. A
considerable number of these myths have been recorded, and they are of great interest as shedding some
light on the primitive beliefs of a wholly primitive
people. Such traditions have unquestionably undergone certain changes in process of transmission, but
the modifications and additions are, I think, less considerable than is commonly believed. The Indian pre-
serves in a remarkable way the tales handed down to

him from his ancestors. To him such traditions have a certain sanctity, and he does not consciously change them. They are, as it were, chapters from his sacred book, and in repeating them he tries to give them exactly as they have been told to him. In receiving these and other traditions from the Indians, I have often been interested to see the pains taken to give each tale in its proper form—to tell the story exactly as it should be told. If in the course of his narration the speaker's memory proves at fault on any point, he will consult authorities, asking the opinions of old men who are best acquainted with the story, refreshing his memory by their assistance, fully discussing the doubtful point, and weighing each remark and suggestion with care before continuing his tale.

The creation stories of the various tribes are quite different, though in those which are akin there is usually more or less similarity. Often the stories are told with much detail.* In some cases the very spot at which their ancestors first had life is described, but in others no locality is assigned to the event. Such stories usually include, besides the mere act of creation, the early history of the tribes, and an account of how his primitive weapons and some instruction as to the manner of using them were given to early man.

Sometimes the fact of creation is given in general terms only, or again the material used, and the different acts performed in shaping man and giving him life are described with some minuteness. On the other hand, the earliest stories that we have of some tribes describe them as already existing, but in some far-away

---

*See The Blackfoot Genesis. Blackfoot Lodge Tales, p. 137.

place, or perhaps under the ground, or beneath the surface of a lake.

Such tales, bearing as they usually do on the first acts of the Creator, who is the principal God, have an intimate connection with the religious beliefs of the tribes, and are a part of their religious history. In an article* published in 1893 I gave the creation myth of the Pawnees. I quote the substance of it here:

Tiráwa is the Creator. He made the mountains, the prairies, and the rivers.

The men of the present era were not the original inhabitants of the earth. They were preceded by another race—people of great size and strength. These were so swift of foot, and so powerful, that they could easily run down and kill the buffalo. A great bull was readily carried into camp on the back by these giants, and when a calf or a yearling was killed, the man thrust its head under his belt and carried it dangling against his leg, as the men of to-day carry a rabbit. Often when these people overtook a buffalo they would strike it with their hands, or kick it with the foot, to knock it down, and to-day, the Arikaras say, you can see the marks of these blows—the prints of the hands and the feet—on the flesh of the buffalo beneath the skin, where these people kicked and scratched the animals.

The race of giants had no respect for the Ruler. On the contrary, they derided and insulted him in every way possible. When the sun rose, or when it thundered and rained, they would defy him. They had great confidence in their own powers, and believed that they were able to cope with the Creator. As they

---

*Journal of American Folk-Lore, vol. vi, p. 113, 1893.

increased in numbers they grew more defiant, and at length became so bad that *Tiráwa* determined to destroy them. This he attempted to do at first by shooting the lightning at them; but the bolts glanced aside from their bodies without injuring them. When he found that they could not be killed by that means, he sent a great rain, which destroyed them by drowning. The ground became water-soaked and soft, and these large and heavy people sank into it and were engulfed in the mire. The great fossil bones of mastodons, elephants, and *Brontotheridœ* are said to be the bones of these giants; and that such remains are often found sticking out of cut banks, or in deep cañons, buried under many feet of earth, is deemed conclusive evidence that the giants did sink into the soft earth and so perish.

After the giant race had passed away, *Tiráwa* created a new people, a man and a woman, who were like those now on the earth. These people were at first poor, naked, and were without any knowledge of how they should live; but after a time the Creator gave them the corn, the buffalo, and the wild roots and fruits of the prairie for food, bows and arrows to kill their game, and fire sticks to furnish a means of cooking it. The Ruler provided for them these various things, such as trees bearing fruits, and things that grow in the ground, artichokes, wild turnips, and other roots. In the rivers he put fish, and on the land game. All these things, everything good to eat found on the plains or in the timber, was given to them by *Tiráwa*.

All these gifts were presented to the Pawnees in the country in which they were originally created, and which, as clearly appears from the statements of the oldest men, was far to the southwest. It was in this original country that the Pawnees received their sacred bundles. When they were given them, the people knew nothing of iron, but used flint knives and arrowheads. The bundles are said to have been handed down from the Father, though in certain cases, special stories are told how particular bundles came to be received.

A more detailed account of the creation and the doings of the original people is given by the Arikaras, but it is not in all respects like that told by the Pawnees, for these two tribes, though belonging to the same family, separated long ago. This story, which is generally known in the Arikara tribe, has come to me from various sources. Two Crows—the chief priest and the fountain of sacred learning for the tribe —Pahukatawá, Fighting Bear, and others have given me portions of this history; but the most complete account I owe to the kindness of the Rev. C. L. Hall, who had it from a Ree known as Peter Burdash, and he received it direct from Ka-ka-pit'ka (Two Crows), the priest. The account is as follows: In the beginning *Atiuch* (= Pawnee *Atíus*) created the earth and a people of stone. These people were so strong that they had no need of the Creator, and would not obey him. They even defied him; so he determined to put an end to them. He therefore caused a great rain, which fell continuously for many days, until the land was all covered with water, and the trees were dead and the tops of the hills were submerged. Many of these people being big and heavy, and so able to move only slowly, could not reach the tops of the hills, to which all tried to escape for safety, and even those who did so were drowned by the rising waters, which at last covered the whole land. Everything on the earth was dead. To-day in the washed clay bluffs of the bad lands the horizontal lines of stratification are shown as marking the level of the waters at various times during this flood, and the hard sandstone pinnacles which cap the bluffs, and which sometimes present a rude semblance of the human form, are pointed out as the remains of these giants.

Now when everything was dead, there were left a mosquito flying about over the water and a little duck swimming on it. These two met, and the duck said to the mosquito, "How is it that you are here?" The mosquito said, "I can live on this foam; how is it with you?" The duck answered, "When I am hungry, I can dive down and eat the green weed that grows under the water." Then said the mosquito: "I am tired of this foam. If you will take me with you to taste of the things of the earth, I shall know that you are true." So the duck took the mosquito under his wing, where he would keep dry, and dived down with him to the bottom of the water, and as soon as they touched the ground all the water disappeared. There was now nothing living on the earth.

Then *Atíuch* determined that he would again make men, and he did so. But again he made them too nearly like himself. They were too powerful, and he was afraid of them, and again destroyed them all.

Then he made one man like the men of to-day. When, this man had been created he said to himself: "How is it now? There is still something that does not quite please me." Then *Atíuch* made a woman, and set her by the man, and the man said: "You knew why I was not pleased. You knew what I wanted. Now I can walk the earth in gladness."

Atiuch seems to have made men and the animals up above in the sky where he lives, and when he was satisfied with what he had made, he resolved to place them upon the earth. So he called the lightning to put them on the earth, and the lightning caused a cloud to come, and the cloud received what *Atiuch* had made. But the lightning, acting as he always does, set them down on the earth with a crash, and as the ground was still wet with the water that had covered it, they all sank into the soft earth. This made the lightning feel very badly, and he cried; and to this day, whenever he strikes the earth, he cries. That is what we hear when it thunders.

Now all living things were under the ground in confusion and asking one another what each was; but one day, as the mole was digging around, he broke a hole through, so that the light streamed in, and he drew back frightened. He has never had any eyes since; the light put them out. The mole did not want to come out, but all the others came out on to the earth through the hole the mole had made.

After they had come out from the ground, the people looked about to see where they should go. They had nothing. They did not know what to do, nor how to support themselves. They began to travel, moving very slowly; but after their third day's camp a boy, who had been left behind asleep at the first camp that they had made, overtook the company, carrying in his arms a large bundle. The people asked him what this was. He replied that when he woke up and found the people gone, he cried to Father for help, and Father gave him this bundle, which had taught him to find the way to his people.

Then the people were glad, and said that now they would find the way, and they went on.

After they had gone a long way, they came to a deep ravine with high steep banks, and they could not cross it. There they had to stop. All came to this place, but they could not get over it. They asked the boy what they should do, and he opened the bundle, and out of it came a bird with a sharp bill *—the most sacred of all birds, the bone striker. Wherever this bird strikes its bill, it makes a hole. This bird flew over the ravine and began to strike the bank with his bill, and flew against the bank again and again, and at last the dirt fell down and filled up the ravine and made a road for the people to pass across. A part of them passed over, but before all had crossed, the road closed up, and the ravine became as it had been at first. Those who were behind perished. They were changed into badgers, snakes, and animals living in the ground. They went on further, and at length came to a thick wood —so thick that they could not pass through it. Here they had to stop, for they did not know how they could get through this timber. Again they asked the boy what should be done, and he opened the bundle, and an owl came out from it and went into the wood and made a path through it. A number of the people got through the wood, but some old women and poor children were lagging behind, and the road closed up and caught them, and these were changed to bears, wildcats, elks, and so on.

The people went on further, and came to a big river which poured down and stopped them, and they

---

*This is thought to be a woodpecker (*Colaptes*).

waited on the bank. When they went to the bundle, a big hawk came out of it. This bird flew across the river and caused the water to stop flowing. They started across the dry river bed, and when part had gone across and were on this side, and some old women and poor children were still in the stream bed, the water began to flow again and drowned them. These people were turned into fishes, and this is why fishes are related to men.

They went on until they came to some high hills called the Blue Mountains, and from these mountains they saw a beautiful country that they thought would be good to live in; but when they consulted the boy who carried the bundle, he said, "No, we shall see life and live in it." So they went on.

Soon after this, some people began to gamble, and one party won everything that the others had, and at last they began to quarrel and then to fight, and the people separated and went different ways, and the animals, which had all this time been with them, got frightened and ran away. But some of the people still remained, and they asked the boy what they should do, and he went to the bundle and took from it a pipe, and when he held up the pipe the fighting ceased. With the pipe was a stone arrowhead, and the boy told them they must make others like this, for from now on they would have to fight; but before this there had been no war. In the bundle they found also an ear of corn. The boy said: "We are to live by this. This is our Mother." The corn taught them how to make bows and arrows.

Now the people no longer spoke one language, and the eight tribes who had run away no longer understood each other and lived together, but wandered about, and the Mother (*Atiná* = Pawnee *Atíra*) no longer remained with them, but left them alone. The ninth or remaining band—which included the Rees, Mandans, and Pawnees—now left the Blue Mountains and travelled on until they reached a great river, and then they knew what the boy meant by saying "We shall see life and live in it." Life meant the Missouri River, and they said, "This is the place where our Mother means us to live." The first night they stayed by the river, but they went off in the morning and left behind them two dogs asleep. One was black, the other white; one was male, the other female. At the third camp they said, "This is a good place; we will live here." They asked the boy what they should do, and he told them that they should separate into three bands; that he would divide the corn among them, and they could plant it. He broke off the nub and gave it to the Mandans, the big end and gave it to the Pawnees, and the middle of the ear he gave to the Rees. To this day the Mandans have the shortest corn, the Rees next in size, and the Pawnees the best and largest. He also took from the bundle beans, which he divided among the people, and the sack of a buffalo's heart full of tobacco. Here by the river they first planted and ate, and were well off, while the eight bands that had run away were dying of hunger. When they got here they had no fire. They knew nothing of it. They tried to get it from the sun, and sent the swallow to bring it. He flew toward the sun, but could not get the fire, and came back saying that the sun had burned him. This is why the swallow's back is black to-day. The crow was sent. He used to be white, but the sun burned him too. Another kind of bird was sent, and he got the fire.

After this they travelled again, and as they travelled they were followed by two great fires, that came up on the hills behind them and shut them in, so that they did not know how to escape. The bundle told them to go to a cedar tree on a precipice, and that if they held fast to this, they would not be hurt by these two great bad things. They did so and escaped, but all cedars have been crooked ever since. These two great fires were the two dogs that had been left behind at their first camp. These dogs then came to them and said: "Our hearts are not all bad. We have bitten you because you left us without waking us up, but now we have had our revenge, and we want to live with you." But sickness and death have followed the people ever since they first left these dogs behind.

The dogs were taken back into the company and grew old. The female dog grew old and poor and died first, and was thrown into the river, and after that the male dog died; but before he died they said to him, "Now you are going to die and be with your wife." "Yes," he replied. "But you will not hate us. From this time you will eat us, and so you will think well of us. And from the female dog's skin has come the squash, and you will like this, and on this account, also, you will not hate us." So ever since that day, dogs have been raised as friends, and afterward eaten for revenge, because of their treachery.

After this, they looked out on the prairie and saw some great black animals having horns, and they looked as though they were going to attack them. The people dug a hole, and got in and covered it over, and when the buffalo rushed on them they were safe, though their dwelling trembled and the people thought the roof would fall in. Finally some one

Pawnee Dirt Lodge

looked out and saw the buffalo standing around. They did not look very fierce, so forty men, women, and children ventured out; but the buffalo attacked them, tore off their arms and ate them, and tore off their hair. Ever since that time there has been a lock of Ree hair in the buffalo's mouth, hanging down from his chin. One handsome young woman was carried off by the buffalo. They held a council to know what they should do with her. She said she could not travel, and they did not wish to kill her. They did not wish to let her go either. But one night, when she was sleeping in the midst of the band, a young bull came to her and pulled her sleeve and told her to follow him, that he would show her the way back to her people. He did so, and his parting words to her were: "Tell your people that we do not like the bows and arrows that they make, and so we have attacked you."*

The young woman was gladly received. They asked the boy with the bundle what should be done with the buffalo. He answered: "The buffalo are to be our food. They ate us first, so now we will always follow them for food. We must make arrows like the

---

*The Algonquin Blackfeet also tell of a time soon after the creation when the buffalo used to eat them. This was before they had bows and arrows; in fact, in some accounts it is even said that then the people had paws like the bears, and supported themselves by digging roots and gathering berries. When *Nápi,* the Blackfoot Creator, learned that the buffalo were killing and eating the people, he felt very badly, and he split their paws so as to make fingers on them, and made bows and arrows and taught the people how to use them. There is also a Blackfoot story of a young woman who was captured and taken away by the buffalo, and who afterward returned to the tribe.—See Blackfoot Lodge Tales, pp. 104 and 140.

one *Tinawá* (= Pawnee *Tiráwa*) gave us with the pipe, and fight the buffalo with them." After making many arrows of the flint they use for striking fires, they all came out of the hole in the earth and lived by planting and hunting.

The Rees have always kept near the Missouri River, and have lived by planting. The bundle reputed to have been given to the boy in the beginning is now in the house of Two Crows. It is still powerful. It contains the ear of corn which was first given to the Rees. When a great young man dies—a chief's son—and the people mourn, the relations are asked to the Ree medicine lodge, and the ear of corn is taken from the bundle, put for a short time in a bucket of water and then replaced in the bundle. As many as drink of that water are cured of sad hearts, and never mourn their friends again.

CHAPTER XII.

THE WORLD OF THE DEAD.

LIKE most people, civilized or savage, the Indian believes in the immortality of the soul. To him the future life is very real, for sometimes—in dreams or during a fainting fit, or in delirium of sickness—visions come to him which he believes are glimpses into the life of another world—a world peopled by the spirits of the departed. It is always difficult to induce the Indian to formulate his views on the future life. Often perhaps he has none, or if he has such beliefs, like our own on the same subject, they are vague and hazy. Besides this, Indians are little accustomed to deal with abstract conceptions, and lack words to express them. Nevertheless, some notion of their beliefs may be gathered from the accounts which they give of ghosts and the ghost country, for all the tribes have tales which speak of the inhabitants of the spirit world, and tell us what they do and how they live. Such stories purport to come from those who have died and have been restored to life again, or from living persons who have visited the country where the spirits dwell, and then returning to their tribe have reported the condition and the ways of the departed.

The views held of this world of the dead differ widely in different tribes. With some it appears to be a real "happy hunting ground," a country of wide green prairies and cool clear streams, where the buffalo and other game are always plenty and fat, where the lodges are ever new and white, the ponies always swift, the war parties successful, and the people happy. Sometimes, even now, the Indian of the south, when the slanting rays of the westering sun tinge the autumnal haze with red, beholds dimly, far away, the white lodges of such a happy camp, and, dazzled by the tinted beams, sees through the mist and dust ghostly warriors returning from the buffalo hunt, leading horses laden as in olden times with dripping meat and with shaggy skins. A speech made by the spirit of a Pawnee woman shows the feeling that these people have about the future life. This woman not long after her death appeared to her husband, who, holding their young child in his arms, was mourning for her, and said: "You are very unhappy here. There is a place to go where we would not be unhappy. Where I have been nothing bad happens to one. Here you never know what evil will come to you. You and the child had better come to me." In the same story father and mother and child at last die, and it is said of them, "They have gone to that place where there is a living"—strong testimony to the Pawnee's faith in a happy future life.*

With other tribes the ghost country is a land of unrealities, where the unhappy shadows endure an existence which is an unsubstantial mockery of this life. Here they hunt shadow buffaloes with arrows, which, on being lifted from the ground, are found to be only blades of grass; their camps or their buffalo traps when approached vanish from sight; or their canoes,

*Pawnee Hero Stories and Folk-Tales, p. 129.

though real to the ghosts, are to mortal eyes rotten, moss-covered and full of holes; their salmon and trout are only dead branches and leaves, floating on the river's current, and even the people themselves, though to all appearance human, turn to skeletons if a word is spoken above a whisper.

To us, who have been reared in the hope of an immortality which promises happiness, there is something inexpressibly pathetic in these vague conceptions of a future life which is so much more miserable than the savage existence in this world, checkered though it is; for even to the savage, while he is still alive, hope always remains. If his camp has been attacked, his people slain, and he himself is a fugitive, hiding from enemies who are eager to take his life, he looks forward to a time when he shall take vengeance for these wrongs and destroy those who have injured him; or if the people are starving, and he sees his wives and little ones wasting away with hunger, he thinks always that to-morrow may bring the buffalo and plenty and contentment. But to this gloomy future life there is no period. It must go on forever.

The melancholy views of a future state held by such tribes as the Blackfeet, the Gros Ventres of the Prairie, the Chinooks, and some other Pacific slope tribes, present singular resemblances to those expressed in the earlier Greek and Roman mythology.

The spirits of the dead take various forms, but they are always unsubstantial as air, though to the eye they may appear real. They are frequently seen by living persons, but are likely to vanish at any moment. The tiny whirlwinds of dust often seen moving about on the prairie in hot summer days are believed by the Pawnees to be ghosts, by other tribes owls are thought to be ghosts. Sometimes spirits take the forms of skeletons, which may be able to walk about, or they may appear as ordinary men and women. It seems possible that these spirits can at will take forms such as please them, and in a specific case a ghost appeared in the form of a bear, and in another it took the shape of a wolf. To see a ghost is by no means an every-day matter. Much more often they are heard to speak or to whistle, and such sounds terrify those who hear them, for the Indians are much afraid of ghosts. Some of these spirits are beneficent, others are harmful, and of the latter, being the more dreaded, much more is heard than of those which wield kindly powers. The hurtful ghosts frighten people by tugging at their blankets while they are walking through the timber at night, or they whistle down the smokehole, or tap on the lodge skins. Such acts, though sufficiently alarming, are not in themselves very serious, and may perhaps be indulged in only for the sake of frightening people. But the spirits that are really inimical do much more terrible things than these. They shoot arrows of disease at people, causing rheumatism, paralysis, St. Vitus's dance, long wasting illness, and oftentimes death.

The actual location of the world of spirits—the home of the dead—varies with the tribe. Many of the peoples of the southern plains believe to-day that this home of the dead is above us, in or above the sky; others hold that it is to the west, beyond the big water; others still think that it is in the south or east. The Blackfeet locate this country of the future close to their present home, in the desolate sandhills south of the Saskatchewan River.

Occasionally, glimpses are seen among some tribes

of a belief in the transmigration of souls. The Kla-
math and Modoc Indians believe that the spirits of
the dead inhabit the bodies of fishes. The ghosts of
medicine men, conjurors, or priests, after death are
often thought to take the shape of an owl—always a
bird of mysterious, if not supernatural, powers—or the
soul of a very brave man might after death inhabit
the body of some brave, fierce animal, like a bear.
Yet this is not supposed to happen commonly, nor do
the helpful animals which so constantly appear in the
folk stories of the Indians ever seem to be the spirits
of those who have lived on earth. These belong to a
class of beings entirely different from mortals.

On the other hand, in the creation story of the
Arikaras, which details also the earlier wanderings of
the first Indians, it is said, as already remarked, that
certain people who were overwhelmed by water, by
land slides, and in forest fallings, were changed into
fishes and various other animals which live principally
under ground or in the woods.

Some Indians believe in reincarnation, the individual at each succeeding birth retaining the sex and
the same peculiar physical characteristics. It is related that a certain chief of the Wrangel Indians
named Harsha, who died about two hundred years
ago, has since been reincarnated five times, and at
each birth is known by the scar of a stab in the right
groin. Another chief, reincarnated three times, is
always recognised by a peculiar lock of gray hair.
These Indians believe that heaven—or the abode of
the spirits—is above us. It is reached by a ladder
and entered through a hole at the point where the
ladder ends.

In almost all the tribes it is believed that per-

sons who have died may, under extraordinary circumstances, become alive again; in other words, that the
ghosts may return from the ghost country to the tribal
home, resuming their mortal shapes, and to all appearance again becoming persons. There seems always a
possibility, however, that such returned ghosts will
vanish on some provocation or other. This idea, which
is found among the tribes of the plains, the mountains, and the Pacific coast, is common to the folk
stories of all races. It is to be remembered, however,
that the story of a ghost who had returned to life
and had afterward, through some fault of relations or
friends, been forced to disappear, would be much more
likely to be preserved in the unwritten literature of a
tribe than one telling of a person who, after having
died, has come to life, and then has remained with the
tribe, living out a full term of years.

I have met several men who believe that they themselves have died, visited the camps of the ghosts, and
then for some reason returned to life and to their
homes, and some of them have related to me what
they had seen in the ghost country. Besides this, I
have been told many other stories, which relate with
more or less detail what is done and said there. A
study of such stories will present as clear an idea of
this future life, and the way it is regarded by the Indians, as can be given in any other way.

Some of these stories resemble in a remarkable degree tales of other lands, which are familiar even to
our children. One of these, told with some detail, is
of singular interest, for it presents a close parallel to
the classical myth of Orpheus and Eurydice, but the
Indian hero was more fortunate than his Old World
prototype, for he was successful in his quest, and re-

covered the wife for whose sake he had faced the hor-
rors of the ghost country and the peril of death.

Interesting in connection with such visits paid by
human beings to the supernatural world are the frequent allusions in these accounts to the peculiar odour
exhaled by living persons. The gods, or the ghosts,
when they come near to the place where the individual
is concealed, often discern his presence by this odour,
and call out, "I smell a person," or "What is this bad
smell?" The burning of sweet grass or sweet pine
usually purifies the air, so that the smell is no longer
complained of.

CHAPTER XIII.

VOLUMES might be written on the Indian religion without exhausting it. The different beliefs of the various tribes, their ceremonial, and the religious history, as given in their traditions, comprise an interesting and difficult study. As a specific example of the religious beliefs of a particular tribe, I quote an account of the Pawnee religion taken from the paper* already mentioned. It gives a somewhat detailed statement of the faith of that people when I first knew them, and before they had been greatly changed by contact with civilization.

The Deity of the Pawnees is *Atíus Tiráwa.*† He is an intangible spirit, omnipotent and beneficent. He pervades the universe, and is its supreme ruler. Upon his will depends everything that happens. He can bring good luck or bad; can give success or failure. Everything rests with him. As a natural consequence of this conception of the Deity, the Pawnees are a very religious people. Nothing is undertaken without a prayer to the Father for assistance. When the pipe is lighted, the first few whiffs are blown to the Deity. When food is eaten, a small portion of it

---

*Journal of American Folk-Lore, vol. vi, p. 113, 1893.
†*Atíus* = father. *Tiráwa* = spirit.

is placed on the ground as a sacrifice to him. He is propitiated by burnt offerings. When they started off on the summer and winter hunts, a part of the first animal which was killed, either a deer or buffalo, was burned to him. The first buffalo killed by a young boy was offered to him. The common prayer among the Pawnees is, "Father, you are the Ruler." They always acknowledge his power and implore his help. He is called "Father, who is above"; "Father, who is in all places."

Tiráwa lives up above in the sky. They say, "The heavens are the house of *Tiráwa,* and we live inside of it." The overarching hemisphere of the sky, which on all sides reaches down to earth at the horizon, in their minds is likened to the walls and roof of the dome-shaped dirt lodges, which the Pawnees inhabit. A similar conception prevails among the Blackfeet.

Next in importance to *Atíus* comes the Earth, which is greatly reverenced. The Pawnees came out of the earth and return to it again. The first whiffs of the pipe are offered to *Atíus,* but after these smokes to him, the next are blown to the earth, and the prayer, "Father of the dead, you see us," is expressed. Not very much is said by the Pawnees about the reverence which they feel for the earth, but much is told about the power of the Mother Corn, "through which they worship," which cares for and protects them, which taught them much that they know, and which, symbolizing the earth, represents in material form something which they revere. A Ree priest said to me: "Just as the white people talk about Jesus Christ, so we feel about the corn." Various explanations are given of the term "Mother," which is applied to the corn, but none are altogether satisfactory. The reference may be to the fact that the corn has always supported and nourished them, as the child is nourished and supported by its mother's milk, or, with a deeper meaning, it may be to the productive power of the earth, which each year brings forth its increase.

The Sun and the Moon and the Stars are personified. They are regarded as people, and prayers are made to them. There is some reason for believing that the sun and the moon once occupied a more important position in the Pawnee religious system than they do to-day. There are some songs which refer to the Sun as the Father and the Moon as the Mother, as if the sun represented the male and the moon the female principle. *O-pi-ri-kus,* the Morning Star, is especially revered by the Skidi, and human sacrifices were made to it.

It is represented that each day or night the Sun, Moon, and Stars paint themselves up and start out on a journey, returning to their respective lodges after their course is accomplished. There are two or three versions of a story which tells of a young woman taken up from earth by a Star and married to him. This young woman lived up in heaven for a time, but was killed while attempting to escape to earth again. Her child—the son of the Star—reached the earth, and lived long in the tribe. He had great power, which he derived from his father.

The Thunder is reverenced by the Pawnees, and a special ceremony of sacrifice and worship is performed at the time of the first thunder in spring, which tells them that the winter is at an end, and that the season for planting is at hand.

The various wild animals are regarded as agents or servants of *Atius,* and are known as *nahúrac,* a word which means animal. It does not refer particularly to these magical or mystical animals which are the Deity's servants, but is a general term applied to any fish, reptile, bird, or beast. The *nahúrac* personify the various attributes of *Atius.* He uses them as his messengers, and they have great knowledge and power, which they derive from him. They hold a relation to the supreme power very similar to that of the angels in the Old Testament. The animals which possess these peculiar powers are, of course, not real animals. They are—we may presume—spirits who assume these shapes when they appear to men. Sometimes, or in some of the stories, they are represented as changing from the animal shape to that of men—as in the account of the origin of the Young Dog's Dance.*

Perhaps no one at the present day could specify the precise attributes of each of the different *nahúrac,* hut there are certain characteristics which are well known to pertain to some of them.

Of all the animals, none was so important to the Pawnees as the buffalo. It fed and clothed them, and, with their corn, was all their support. This alone was enough to entitle it to a very high place in their esteem. It was a sacred animal of great power, and was a favourite secret helper, and although it did not receive a measure of reverence equal to that felt for the Mother Corn, it was yet the most sacred and highly respected of all the animals. The eidolon of the buffalo—its skull—occupied a prominent position

---

*Journal of American Folk-Lore, vol. iv, p. 307.

in many of the Pawnee sacred ceremonies, and rested on the top of many a lodge, signifying that it was the special helper of the owner. Even to-day, although the buffalo has long been extinct, everywhere in the Ree village this same object may be seen, at once the relic of a noble animal which has disappeared from the land, and the symbol of a faith which is passing away with the passing of a people. The buffalo appears to have typified force or power, as well as the quality of dashing blindly onward. Besides this, there were some buffaloes which were invulnerable, which could not be killed by ordinary weapons. It was necessary to rub on the arrow used against them, or in later times on the bullet, a peculiar potent medicine before the missile would penetrate the skin. Such buffaloes were usually described as sexless, of enormous size, and without joints in their legs.

While the bear was by no means so sacred as the buffalo, he was regarded as singular for wisdom and power. He symbolizes invulnerability. He knows how to cure himself. No matter how badly he may be wounded, if only a little breath is left in his body he can heal himself. It is said that sometimes he does this by plugging up with certain medicine herbs the wounds which have been inflicted on him. He has also the power of breathing out from his nostrils different-coloured dusts—red, blue, and yellow—or of spitting out different-coloured earths. Certain medicine bears which belonged to two of the bands could not be wounded by ball or arrow. Of one of these it was said, "The lead will flatten out, the spike (of the arrow) will roll up" when it strikes his body.

The beaver was regarded as an animal of great wisdom and power, and a beaver was always one of the four chiefs who ruled the councils of the *nahúrac.* Craft was typified in the wolf; courage, fierceness, or success in war by the birds of prey, the eagle standing at the head; the deer stood for fleetness, etc.

The black eagle, the white-headed eagle, and the buzzard are messengers of *Tiráwa;* by them he sent his orders to the first high priest, and instructed him in the secrets of his priestship and in the other secrets. The buzzard and the white-headed eagle represent the old men—those who have little hair and those whose hair is white; it is from these ancient men that the secrets have been handed down from generation to generation.

The *nahúrac* had an organization and methods of conveying information to favoured individuals. They had meeting places where they held councils which were presided over by chiefs. The meeting places were in underground lodges or caves, and there were known to the Pawnees, when they lived in their old home in Nebraska, no less than five such places. These were at $Pa\text{-}h\breve{u}k$, under the high bluff opposite Fremont, Nebraska; at $Ah\text{-}ka\text{-}w\breve{t}t'ak\breve{o}l$, under a high white bluff at the mouth of the Cedar River; at $La\text{-}la\text{-}wa\text{-}koh't\bar{\imath}\text{-}t\bar{o}.$, under an island in the Platte River opposite the Lone Tree (now Central City, Nebraska); under the Sacred Spring $K\bar{\imath}tz\text{-}a\text{-}w\bar{\imath}tz'\breve{u}k$, on the Solomon River in Kansas; and at $Pah\bar{u}'r$, or Guide Rock, in Kansas.

Persons who were pitied by the *nahúrac* were sometimes taken into the lodges, where their cases were discussed in council, and they were helped, and power and wisdom were given them by the animals. After it had been determined that he should thus be helped, the various animals, one after another, would rise in their places and speak to the man, each one giving him the power which was peculiar to itself. In such a council the buffalo would often give the man the power of running over those opposed to him: "You shall run over your enemies, as I do over mine." The bear would give him the power to heal himself if wounded and to cure others. The eagle would give him his own courage and fierceness: "You shall kill your enemies, as I do mine." The wolf would give him the power to creep right into the midst of the enemy's camp without being seen. The owl would say to him, "You shall see in the night as I do"; the deer, "You shall run as fast as I can." So it would go on around the circle, each animal giving him that power or that knowledge which it typified. The speeches made in such *nahúrac* councils were similar in character to those which would be made in any council of men.

Usually much of the knowledge taught a person, who was being helped by the *nahúrac,* was that of the doctors, and those who had received this help were able to perform all those wonderful feats in the doctor's dances for which the Pawnees were so justly renowned. Often, too, these persons were made invulnerable, so that the arrows or the bullets of the enemy would not penetrate their flesh.

The stay of the individuals who might be taken into the *nahúrac* lodges did not, as a rule, last longer than four days, though often a man who had been once received there might come again. If the time mentioned was not long enough to enable him to acquire all the knowledge of the *nahúrac,* it sometimes happened that after such a visit the various animals would meet the person singly out in the hills or on the prairie, and would there communicate to him additional knowledge, especially that touching on the efficacy of various roots and herbs used in healing.

It is to be noted that the *nahúrac* did not content themselves with giving to the person whom they pitied help, and nothing more. They also gave him good advice, telling him to trust always in the Ruler, and to look to One above, who is the giver of all power. Often they explained that all their power came from *Atíus,* whose servants they were; that they did not make themselves great, that they were mortal, and there would be an end to their days.

It is not always specified what shape was taken by the four chiefs who ruled the *nahúrac* councils; but in at least one story it is stated that these were a beaver, an otter, a sandhill crane, and a garfish. In another story a dog appears to have been the chief. These animal councils had a servant who acted as their messenger, and carried word from one *nahúrac* lodge to another. This bird is described with some detail in more than one of the Pawnee stories, and was evidently a species of tern.

The animals were the usual medium of communication between *Atíus* and man. They most often appeared to persons in sleep, telling them what to do, giving them good advice, and generally ordering their lives for them. But there is one story in which an individual is said to have spoken face to face with the Father.

The four cardinal points were respected by the Pawnees, and their place was high, although they were not often spoken of, except in prayers. Still, the formula in smoking was to blow first four smokes to *Atíus,* then four to the earth, and last of all to each of the cardinal points. The east represented the night, for it is from that direction that the darkness comes. So, in one of the stories, a speaker, in advising a young man as to how he should act, says of smoking: "And always blow four smokes to the east, to the night; for in the night something may come to you which will tell you a thing which will happen," that is, come true. It would be hard to find a closer parallel to our saying, "The night brings counsel." It is worthy of note that this conception of the east is the absolute reversal of our notion that the east brings the light—the morning; one of the most familiar figures in our literature.

Closely connected with their respect for the night is their firm confidence in dreams, which to a great extent govern their lives. Their belief in a future life is in part founded on dreams which they have had of being themselves dead, and finding themselves in villages where they recognised among the inhabitants relations and acquaintances who had long been dead. The faith in another life after this one is ended is exemplified by stories already published, which tell of the coming to life of persons who have died, and is fortified by the experiences of certain living men who believe themselves once to have died and visited these villages of the dead.

Prayers for direct help are, as a rule, made only to the Father, and not to the animals, nor to the Sun, Moon, and Stars. But the last are constantly implored to act as intercessors with *Atius* to help the people. A prayer frequently made to the animals by a person in distress was this: "If you have any power, intercede for me." It is constantly stated in the tales current among the Pawnees that in minor matters the animals may be depended on for help, but if anything very difficult is sought, the petitioner must look only to the Father. The animals seem in many ways to hold a position in the Pawnee religious system analogous to that of the saints in the Roman Catholic faith.

Something must be said about the sacred bundles which are to the Pawnees what the Ark of the Covenant was to the ancient Israelites. Concerning these I may quote what has been written:

"In the lodge or house of every Pawnee of influence, hanging on the west side, and so opposite the door, is the sacred bundle, neatly wrapped in buckskin, and black with smoke and age. What these bundles contain we do not know. Sometimes, from the ends, protrude bits of scalps, and the tips of pipestems and slender sticks; but the whole contents of the bundle are known only to the priests and to its owner—perhaps not always even to him. The sacred bundles are kept on the west side of the lodge, because, being thus furthest from the door, fewer people will pass by them than if they were hung in any other part of the lodge. Various superstitions attach to these bundles. In the lodges where certain of them are kept it is forbidden to put a knife in the fire; in others, a knife may not be thrown; in others, it is not permitted to enter the lodge with the face painted; or, again, a man cannot go in if he has feathers tied in his head.

"No one knows whence the bundles came. Many of them are very old; too old, even, to have a history. Their origin is lost in the haze of the long ago. They say: 'The sacred bundles were given us long ago. No one knows when they came to us.'"

15

It is to be observed that the miracles which so frequently occur in the heroic myths of the Pawnees, and which generally result in the bringing to life of the person who is pitied by the *nahúrac,* often take place during a storm of rain accompanied by wind and thunder. Examples of this are found in the stories of the Dun Horse, Pahukátawa, Ore ke ráhr, and others. The rain, the wind, and the thunder may be regarded as special manifestations of the power of the Deity, or these may perhaps be considered as veils which he uses to conceal the manifestations of this power from the eyes of men.

What has already been said shows that the mythology of the Pawnees inculcates strongly the religious idea, and impresses upon the listener the importance of trusting in the Ruler and asking his help.

Perhaps the most singular thing about this Pawnee religion, as it has been taught to me, is its close resemblance in many particulars to certain forms of the religion of Christ as it exists to-day. While their practices were those of a savage people, their theories of duty and their attitude toward the Supreme Being were on a much more lofty plane. The importance of faith in the Deity is most strongly insisted on; sacrifices must be made to him—offerings of the good things of this earth, often of parts of their own bodies; penance must be done. But, above all things else, those who desire success in life must humble themselves before the Deity and must implore his help. The lessons taught by many of the myths are precisely those which would be taught by the Christian priest to-day, while the burnt-offerings to *Atíus* may be compared with like sacrifices spoken of in the Old Testament, and the personal tortures undergone during certain of their ceremonies are almost the exact equivalents of the sufferings inflicted on themselves by certain religionists of the middle ages.

On the whole, the Pawnee religion, so far as I understand it, is a singularly pure faith, and in its essential features will compare favourably with any savage system. If written in our own sacred books, the trust and submission to the will of the Ruler shown in some of the myths, which I have elsewhere recorded, would be called sublime. What, for example, could be finer than the prayer offered by a man who, through the hostility of a rival, is in the deepest distress and utterly hopeless of human aid, and who throws himself on the mercy of the Creator, and at the same time implores the intercession of the *nahúrac?* This man prepares to offer his horse as a sacrifice to the animals, but before killing it he says: "My Father [who dwells] in all places, it is through you that I am living. Perhaps it was through you that this man put me in this condition. You are the Ruler. Nothing is impossible to you. If you see fit, take this [trouble] away from me. Now you, all fish of the rivers, and you, all birds of the air, and all animals that move upon the earth, and you, O Sun! I present to you this animal. You birds in the air, and you animals upon the earth, we are related; we are alike in this respect, that one Ruler made us all. You see me, how unhappy I am. If you have any power, intercede for me."

CHAPTER XIV.

THE OLD FAITH AND THE NEW.

No subject is more difficult than the religion of a savage people. It is not always easy to determine just what are the beliefs of a civilized race. Certain marked differences between various sects, and the form and ritual of each, may be described with more or less accuracy, but the actual beliefs are hardly to be arrived at. This is partly because most people do not themselves know what they believe—or at least have never put in words all the points of their faith—and also because no two individuals have precisely the same belief.

We have been told of late years that there is no evidence that any tribe of Indians ever believed in one overruling power, yet in the early part of the seventeenth century Jesuits and Puritans alike testified that tribes which they met believed in a god, and it is certain that at the present time many tribes worship a Supreme Being who is the Ruler of the universe.

In the case of many of these tribes this god lives up above in the sky in what we would call heaven, but sometimes his abiding place is under the ground or again at the different cardinal points. The Pawnees, as already stated, now locate him above, yet one story which they tell places him in the west beyond the big water. In the same region is the dwelling-place

Group of Sapelelle La Tetes, West Coast Vancouver Island

of the Sun, the chief Blackfoot god. Other tribes place their principal god in the east, and often his home is beyond the big water which surrounds the continent. Some tribes west of the Rockies worship the Wolf as chief god and creator.

I am inclined to believe that many of the tribes of this continent once worshipped the Sun—as some still do—or perhaps originally the light or the dawn was the god. The prayer of the Blackfoot invariably begins, "Hear Sun, hear Old Man, Above People listen, Under-water People listen." This might fairly be called a prayer to the Sun as the supreme ruler, but also an appeal to all the powers of Nature as well. A Pawnee prayer already quoted reverses this order, and is addressed more specifically to "You all fish of the rivers, you all birds of the air, and all animals that move upon the earth, and you, O Sun!"

In cases where the Sun is the Supreme Father, or old man, the Moon is often the sun's wife, the mother, the old woman; or, on the other hand, the Earth may be the mother. In any case it is true that all tribes have a great reverence for the earth, which they regard as the producer not only of themselves but of all food, the fruitful one, from whom comes all their support. But this is an idea which is as broad as humanity; witness our own figure of Mother Earth. In fact, with many tribes the earth seems to rank as the second of the powers or influences that are prayed to, and in smoking, though the first smoke and prayer is offered to the power above, the second is almost invariably blown downward to the earth. In like manner, while some tribes in blessing or in healing hold up the palms of the hands to the sunlight before passing them over the person to be blessed or the part to be cured, others, as the Cheyennes, place the palms upon the ground, as if the good influence was to be derived from the earth.

Besides the sun, moon, and earth, certain of the stars are held in especial reverence, and this is true particularly of the morning star, which by the Blackfeet is called Early Riser, and is believed to be the son of the Sun and Moon. The Skidi, as has elsewhere been stated, made special sacrifices to this planet, which they believed to have great influence over their crops. Many of the tribes have names for the planets, the brighter stars, and the more important constellations, and relate stories to account for their existence or for the grouping of the stars. Thus the Great Bear is called the Seven Persons by the Blackfeet, and Broken Back by the Arapahoes; the Pleiades, the Seven Stars by Pawnees and Blackfeet, Grouped Together Stars by the Cheyennes. Venus is known by the Cheyennes as "Belonging to the Moon." The Milky Way is called Spirit Road by the Cheyennes, and is the road travelled by the spirits of the departed on their way to the future world. The Blackfeet call it the Wolf Road, and believe it the short trail from the Sun's lodge to this world. Most tribes call it the Ghost's Road.

Besides such intangible and all-pervading spirits as the Spirit Father of the Pawnees, already mentioned, and the heavenly bodies, there are many supernatural agencies of another and secondary class, which are often spoken of as minor gods, but which seem rather to occupy a position corresponding very closely to the saints and angels of our religious system. To such agencies—all of them subordinate to the supreme power—prayers are offered in much the same way that for many centuries petitions have been made by certain sects of the Christian religion to saints and holy personages. These agencies, which often assume a material shape, and which appear to men in the form of beasts, birds, rocks, buttes, or mountains, sometimes represent certain forces of Nature, or again only qualities or powers, mental or physical. These forces or qualities do not, however, invariably take a visible shape; and although the thunder is believed by many tribes to have the form of a bird, there are others by which it has never been seen.

In all the important affairs of life help is asked of these supernatural agencies; prayers are made to them and sacrifices offered—a puff of smoke, a little food, or a bit of tobacco or red cloth. They occupy the position of intercessors, mediators between man and the supreme power. The different classes of these supernatural agencies which appear to inhabit the air and sky above, the world about us and the world beneath us, have already been referred to. They have the power to give to favoured ones the special qualities which each represents, and, besides, to implore for him the help of the Deity. To the man who fasted and dreamed for power, and who—steadfastly enduring the hunger and thirst and the frightful visions which so often caused him to give up the attempt—bore all this suffering to the end, one of these supernatural agencies would often appear as his struggle drew to a close, and though at first perhaps seeming severe and stern, would at length soften and become more kindly, and would then offer wise counsel and friendly advice, promising to give him its power and to help him through life. This was the man's secret helper, his "medicine," the special being to whom his prayers were hereafter offered. This is what is meant when an Indian is spoken of as having been "helped by a wolf," a bear, or an eagle.

The Indian, however, does not call this assisting power by any of these names. He usually speaks of it as his dream or sleep, and says, "It came to me in my sleep," or "A spirit told me in my sleep," and the Blackfoot when he prays says, "Listen, my dream." The so-called "medicine" or bundle of sacred things, which many Indians always carry with them is called by the same name. The owner believes these things to have been given him, or that he has been directed to make them by his dream, and such articles, while he has them about his person, protect him from harm. A friend to whom I was once of service afterward gave me his dream. He told me that he had carried it in battle for many years, and that it had always kept him safe. It was a necklace of bear claws and spherical leaden bullets, and was perhaps the most highly valued of all his possessions. Whirlwind, the chief of the Cheyennes, used to tell of the power of his dream—a little hawk which he wore on his war bonnet—which had always protected him in battle, and especially in one fight, when, during a charge on his enemies, who were fighting behind cover, the bullets flew so thick about him that every feather on his bonnet was cut away, yet no ball touched him, nor was the hawk hit.

Instances where men have been struck and knocked down by balls, which yet, on account of the power of this protection, did not enter the flesh or inflict a wound, are commonly spoken of.

It is impossible to state definitely just how these different powers are regarded—whether it is an actual worship that is offered to them; whether, as has been said, "All nature is alive with gods; every mountain, every tree is worshipped, and the commonest animals are objects of adoration"; or whether one supreme god is adored through these various objects and creatures which typify that god's various attributes. Even the Indian himself does not know just which of these is true. Probably the average red man actually worships each such object. At least it is certain that every object in Nature may have its special property or power which is to be reverenced, and perhaps propitiated. Such objects are probably types, an animal, or plant, or butte, standing for a quality, and being reverenced as the material embodiment of that quality. If, for example, the eagle typifies courage and dash in war, young men about to go on the warpath offer prayers and sacrifices to the eagle, asking him to give them some of his bravery. Yet such prayer is not offered to any actual bird but to some representative eagle—perhaps a spiritual one—which stands for bravery; for while many animals stand for qualities or special powers, the actual animals are in no sense sacred. Some tribes teach kindness and consideration to all living things, and forbid their unnecessary destruction; but even these tribes do not regard any animals as sacred in the sense that they are not to be killed when it is necessary. The animals representing these qualities have special powers, they are supernatural, they are nearer the Deity than men, yet they are his servants. Whatever powers they may possess are not created by themselves nor in any sense inherent in them, but have been given to them by the Ruler, and are exercised only by his permission.

The coming of the white man has brought to the Indian—even to him who has not been exposed to the teaching of the missionaries—more or less of skepticism as to his own religion. He believes that all good gifts, whether mental or material, come from the supreme power, and he sees that the white man has a monopoly of such gifts. Hence, in many cases, he has come to think that the white man's god is rich and wise, while the Indian's is poor and foolish. The one taught his children well, and gave them guns, machinery, and money, the power to talk to each other at a distance, the wisdom to know beforehand what to do in certain circumstances, and great shrewdness in all the affairs of life. The other furnished to his children only their simple arms and utensils and the buffalo for their food. These things satisfied the Indian so long as he knew of nothing better, but now that he is wiser, he cannot but feel more or less contempt for a god who could do no more for his children than this, and he does not hesitate to express the contempt which he feels.

On the other hand, this does not make him more ready for conversion to a belief in the white man's religion. This religion offers to him a set of ideas entirely new and entirely different in character from any that he has ever had before, and he cannot at first comprehend them at all. An Indian friend, who had listened long to the arguments of a Christian missionary, spoke to me with severe scorn of the foolishness of the latter's promises of heaven and threats of hell. "How is it possible for me to go up into the sky?" he said. "Have I wings like an eagle to fly away? Or how can I get to that place down below? I have no claws like a badger to dig down through the ground."

The Indians, as has often been pointed out, are essentially a religious people. They realize man's feebleness, his inability to successfully contend with the powers of Nature, and so they ask for the assistance of all those beings whom they believe to have powers greater than themselves. The sacrifices with which they accompany their prayers may vary from a spoonful of food or a bit of calico to a scalp taken in war, a horse, or a piece of flesh cut from the body. An acquaintance of mine, who had lost three fingers from his left hand and two from his right, told me that at different times in the course of seven years he had sacrificed these missing members in the furtherance of a special object, which he at last attained. In one of the Pawnee stories which I have recorded* a father is related to have sacrificed his only son, whom he dearly loved, in the belief that this act would secure divine favour.

There can be no doubt that in many cases the Indian religion of to-day has been greatly influenced by the teachings of Christian missionaries, and this seems to be true of Pacific coast tribes to a much greater degree than of those dwelling on the plains. More than once, when camping with Indians whose home lay on the west side of the Rocky Mountains, I have been impressed by the survival of evidences of Christian teachings among people who have apparently forgotten those teachings, even though some of their forms still persist. And when one sees a wild Indian—one whom he knows to be a thorough pagan—make the sign of the cross before he prays, one cannot but wonder whence came this man's knowledge of God, who told him the story of the cross.

---

*Pawnee Hero Stories and Folk-Tales, p. 161.

Such a sight carries the mind back over the centuries, and makes real to the observer the extent and the permanence of the devoted work done here in America by the black-robed priests who marched with the little steel-clad army of the Conquistadores when, with all the pomp and circumstance of glorious war, they entered Mexico. At first these fathers made their converts by the sword. Later their unflagging zeal and patient faith subdued tribe after tribe, until at length they reached the western ocean. Slowly they spread along the coast, north and south, and to the outlying islands of the sea, and planted the cross deeper and deeper in the wilderness. In trackless deserts, in tangled forests they preached Christ and his kingdom. The wild tribes of the parched cactus plains, the gentle races of the Pueblo villages, the hardy fishermen of the seashore alike yielded to the faith and energy which inspired these ministers of God. Little by little they made their way up the coast—you can trace their progress on the map to-day—San Diego, San Pedro, San Luis, San José, San Francisco, San Juan—ever fighting the battle of the cross, upheld by their faith. The blazing sun of summer poured down upon them his withering heat; they did not blench. The frosts and snows of winter chilled them; they pushed on. Sky-reaching mountains barred their progress; they surmounted them. Floods stood in their way; they crossed them. Painfully, slowly, on foot through an unknown country, in perils of waters, in perils by the heathen, in perils in the wilderness, "in weariness and painfulness, in watchings often, in hunger and thirst, in fastings often, in cold and nakedness," they held their steadfast way. No danger daunted them, no difficulty turned them back. Death did not stop their march. If one faltered and stumbled and fell, another stepped calmly forward and took his place. No need now to look at the means they sometimes employed, nor to remember that among these servants of God all were not alike worthy. Look only at what they accomplished, and remember at what a cost. And though their earnest labours failed to establish here in the new world the religious empire of which they dreamed, yet no doubt each faithful soul had, in the consciousness of duty well performed, his own abundant reward. And although of their teachings in many tribes much or all has been forgotten, still, even now in wild camps in the distant mountains, the sign of the cross and the vesper bell may remind the wanderer of a time, now long past, when faith was strong and men were willing to die for God's glory. There, in such lonely camps among rugged peaks and far from the haunts of men, is still practiced a rite of the Church. There still grows, though stunted, deformed, and changed, the plant whose seed was first sown centuries ago by that devoted band.

CHAPTER XV.

THE COMING OF THE WHITE MAN.

KNOWLEDGE of the white man came to the different tribes of the west at different times, but a century ago most of them knew little of him, and there are many tribes which have had a real intercourse with the whites for a still shorter time. Long before this the Spaniards in the southwest and on the Pacific coast had made their presence felt, but the Indians usually do not consider that Spaniards are of the same race with the people of European origin who came to them from the east, and often they have a special name for them.

Even after the Indians had learned of the existence of white people, they did not at once come into contact with them. It was often quite a long time before they even began to trade with them, and when they did so, it was in a very small way. The first articles traded for were arms, beads, blankets, and the gaudy finery that the savage loves. Horses—which transformed the Indian, which changed him from a mild and peaceful seeker after food to a warrior and a raider—were by many tribes first obtained not directly from the whites, but by barter from those of their own race.

Most tribes still preserve traditions of the time when they met the first white men, as well as of the time when they first saw horses; but in many cases this was so long ago that all details of the occurrence have been lost. It is certain that the Spaniards and their horses had worked their way up the Pacific slope into Oregon and Washington long before there was any considerable influx of white trappers into the plains country and the Rocky Mountains; and that of the western tribes, those which in miles were furthest from Mexico were the last to learn of the whites and their wonderful powers. One of these peoples was the Blackfeet, of whom I have been told by men still living in the tribe that fifty years ago no Blackfoot could count up to ten, and that a little earlier the number of horses in all three tribes of that confederation was very small. Then they had but few guns, and many of them even used still the stone arrowheads and hatchets and the bone knives of their primitive ancestors.

A people whose intercourse with the whites has been so short and, until recent times, so limited, ought to retain some detailed account of their earliest meeting with civilized men, and such a tradition has come to me from John Monroe, a half-breed Piegan, now nearly seventy years old. It tells of the first time the Blackfeet saw white people—a party of traders from the east, either Frenchmen from Montreal, or one of the very earliest parties of Hudson Bay men which ascended the Saskatchewan River. John Monroe first heard the narrative when a boy from a Blood Indian named Sútane, who was then an old man, and Sútane's grandfather was one of the party who met the white people. The occurrence probably took place during the latter half of the eighteenth century.

When this people lived in the north, a party of the

Blackfeet started out to war. They travelled on, always going southward, until they came to a big water. While passing through a belt of timber on the north bank of this river, they came upon what they took for strange beaver work, where these animals had been cutting down the trees. But on looking closely at the cuttings, they saw that the chips were so large that it must have been an animal much bigger than a beaver that could open its mouth wide enough to cut such chips. They did not understand what this could be, for none of them had ever seen anything like it before. Each man expressed his mind about this, and at last they concluded that some great under-water animal must have done it. At one place they saw that the trunk of a tree was missing, and found the trail over the ground where it had been dragged away from the stump. They followed this trail, so as to see where the animals had taken the log, and what they had done with it, and as they went on, they found many other small trails like this one, all leading into one larger main trail. They then saw the footprints of persons, but they were prints of a foot shaped differently from theirs. There was a deep mark at the heel; the tracks were not flat like those made by people.*

They followed the trail, which kept getting larger and wider as it went. Every little while, another trail joined it. When they came to where they could look through the timber, they saw before them a little open spot on the bank of the river. They looked through the underbrush, and saw what they at first thought

---

*This deep mark was no doubt the imprint of the heel of a shoe.

were bears, and afterward took to be persons, lifting logs and putting them up in a large pile. They crept closer, to where they could see better, and then concluded that these were not people. They were very woolly on the face. Long masses of hair hung down from their chins. They were not clothed—wore no robes. The Blackfeet said: "Why, they have nothing on! They are naked!" Some of them said, "Those are *Súye tuppi*" (water people). They stole around to another point of the timber, still nearer, where they could see better. There they came close to one of these people alone. He was gathering sticks and putting them in a pile. They saw that the skin of his hands and face was white. This one had no hair on his face.* So they said: "Well, this must be a she water animal. The he ones have hair on the face, and the she ones do not."

The oldest man of the party then said: "We had better go away. Maybe they will smell us or feel us here, and perhaps they will kill us, or do something fearful. Let us go." So they went away.

When they got back to their camp, they told what they had seen; that to the south they had found animals that were very much like people—water animals. They said that these animals were naked. That some of them had red bodies,† and some were black all over, except a red mark around the bodies and a fine red tail.‡ Moreover, these people wore no robes or leggings and no breech-clouts.

---

*This was probably a boy gathering poles for roofing.

†Wore red shirts.

‡The old Hudson Bay men used to wear about the waist a red sash the ends of which hung down in front. When they were working, to get these ends out of the way, they would pass

This description caused a great excitement in the camp. Some thought that the strange beings were water animals, and others that they were a new people. All the men of the camp started south to see what this could be. Before they left the camp, the head man told them to be very careful in dealing with the animals, not to interfere with them nor to get in their way, and not to try to hurt them nor to anger them.

The party started, and when they reached the opening, the animals were still there at work. After they had watched them for some time the head man of the party said to the others: "All you stay here, and I will go down to them alone. If they do nothing to me you wait here, but if they attack or hurt me, you rush on them, and we will fight hard, and try not to let them capture any of us." The man started, and when he came close to the corner of the houses he stood still. One of the men, who was working near by, walked up to him, looked him straight in the face, and stretched out his arm. The Indian looked at him, and did not know what he wanted. Some more of the men came up to him, and the Indian saw that all of them were persons like himself, except that they were of a different colour and had a different voice. The hair on their faces was fair.

When the other Indians saw that no harm had been done to their leader, some of them went down to him, one by one, and by twos and threes, but most of the party remained hidden in the timber. They were still afraid of these strange new beings.

---

them around the body and under the sash, so that they hung down behind.

The whites spoke to them, and asked them to come into the house, making motions to them, but the Indians did not understand what was meant by these signs. The whites would walk away, and then come back and take hold of the Indians' robes and pull them. At last some of the Blackfeet followed the white men into the house. Those who had gone in came back and told the others strange stories of the wonderful things they had seen in this house. As they gained confidence, many others went in, while still others would not go in, nor would they go close to the new people.

The whites showed them a long and curious-looking piece of wood. They did not know of what kind of stone one part of it was made. It was hard and black. The white man took down from the wall a white cow's horn and poured out some black sand into his hand, and poured it down into a hole in this long stick. Then he took a little bunch of grass and pushed this into the hole with another stick, then measured with his fingers the length of the stick left out of the hole. Then he took a round thing out of a bag, and put it into the hole, and put down some more fine grass. Then he poured out some more of the black sand into the side of the stick. The Indians stood around, taking great interest in the way the man was handling this stick. The white man now began to make all kinds of signs to the Indians, which they did not understand. Sometimes he would make a big sound with his mouth, and then point to the stick. He would put the stick to his shoulder, holding it out in front of him, and make a great many motions. Then he gave it to one of the Indians. He showed him the under parts, and put his finger there. The Indian touched the under part and the stick went off in the air and made a thundering sound, a terrible crash. The Indian staggered back, and the others were very much scared. Some dropped to the ground, while all the whites laughed and shook their heads at them. All laughed, and made many signs to the Blackfeet, none of which they understood. The white man took down the horn of black sand, and again did these things to the stick, but this time the Indians all stood back. They were afraid. When he had finished the motions, the white man invited them out of doors. Then he sat down, and took aim at a log lying on the ground. The same great thunder sounded. He walked up to the log, showed the bullet hole, and pushed a little stick into it; then he loaded the gun again.

By this time the Indians were beginning to understand the power of the stick. After the white man had loaded it, he handed the gun to the Indian, took him close to the log, showed him how to aim the gun and how to pull the trigger. The Indian fired and hit the log.

The white men showed these Blackfeet their knives, whittling sticks with them, and showing them how well they could cut. The Indians were very much delighted with the power of these knives. Then they saw a big, woolly white man standing out in front of the house, and he with his axe would cut a big log in two in only a short time. All these things were very strange to them. The white men looked closely at the Blackfoot war dresses and arms and wanted them, and gave their visitors some knives and copper cups for their dresses and the skins that they wore. The visitors stayed with the white men some days, camping near by. They kept wondering at these people, at how they looked, the things which they had, and what they did. The white men kept making signs to them, but they understood nothing of it all.

After a time the Blackfeet returned to their camp. Afterward, many others visited the whites, and this was the beginning of a friendly intercourse between the two peoples. After a time they came to understand each other a little, and trade relations were opened. The Indians learned that they could get the white man's things in exchange for the skins of small animals, and they began to trade and to get guns. It was when they got these arms that they first began to take courage, and to go out of the timber on to the prairie toward the mountains. In those old days the Hudson Bay traders used to tell the Indians to bring in the hair from the skins of buffalo, to put it in sacks and bring it in to trade. They did so, but all of a sudden the traders would take no more buffalo hair.

This probably refers to the attempt made during the last century in the Selkirk settlement to establish a corporation for making cloth from buffalo hair.

Of the special articles brought by the white men, the first to exercise an important influence on the people were horses. The possession of these animals greatly increased their liberty, stimulated them to wars with their neighbours, and in fact wrought a most important change in the character of the people.* The knowledge of the horse advanced from the south northward, and these animals spread northward

---

*Blackfoot Lodge Tales, p. 242.

up the Pacific coast more rapidly than on the east side of the mountains. The tribes of the southern plains— Comanches, Kiowas, Wichitas, Arapahoes, Navajoes, and others—obtained horses very early. The Pawnees and various tribes of the Dakotas later. The Utes, Snakes, and Kutenais had horses early; and the last of the plains tribe to obtain them were the Blackfeet, Assiniboines, and Plains Crees. In the case of tribes that have long had horses, it is impossible to even approximate the date at which they were obtained—it happened too long ago—but with the more northern tribes, which have had horses for a short time only, I have been more successful in my inquiries, and from several old men among the Piegans I have accounts of the first coming of horses.

As I have said, many myths exist to account for the coming of the horse, but this Piegan testimony is that of an eye-witness. Wolf Calf is probably over one hundred years old. He well remembers when the first white men passed through the country, and old men of seventy years or thereabouts tell me that he was a proved warrior when they were little boys. He believes that he was born in 1793. From him I have definite and detailed accounts of the ways of the Piegans in days before they had been at all influenced by civilized man. I believe his statements to be as worthy of credence as any can be which depend solely on memory. The account which follows is a translation of his narrative, taken down from his own lips some years ago. He said:

"Long ago, when I was young, just getting big enough to use a bow, we used arrowpoints of stone. Then the knives were made of flint. Not long after this, arrowpoints of sheet iron began to come into use.

After we used the stone knives, we began to get white men's knives. The first of these that we had were made of a strip of tin. This was set into a bone, so that only a narrow edge of the tin protruded, and this was sharpened and used for skinning.

"Before that time the Piegans had no horses. When they moved their camp they packed their lodges on dogs.

"The first horses we ever saw came from west of the mountains. A band of the Piegans were camped on Belly River, at a place that we call 'Smash the Heads,' where we jumped buffalo. They had been driving buffalo over the cliff here, so that they had plenty of meat.

"There had come over the mountains to hunt buffalo a Kutenai who had some horses, and he was running buffalo; but for some reason he had no luck. He could kill nothing. He had seen from far off the Piegan camp, but he did not go near it, for the Piegans and the Kutenais were enemies.

"This Kutenai could not kill anything, and he and his family had nothing to eat and were starving. At last he made up his mind that he would go into the camp of his enemies and give himself up, for he said, 'I might as well be killed at once as die of hunger.' So with his wife and children he rode away from his camp up in the mountains, leaving his lodge standing and his horses feeding about it, all except those which his woman and his three children were riding, and started for the camp of the Piegans.

"They had just made a big drive, and had run a great lot of buffalo over the cliff. There were many dead in the pískun, and the men were killing those that were left alive, when suddenly the Kutenai, on his horse, followed by his wife and children on theirs, rode over a hill near by. When they saw him, all the Piegans were astonished and wondered what this could be. None of them had ever seen anything like it, and they were afraid. They thought it was something mysterious. The chief of the Piegans called out to his people: 'This is something very strange. I have heard of wonderful things that have happened from the earliest times until now, but I never heard of anything like this. This thing must have come from above (i.e., from the sun), or else it must have come out of the hill (i.e., from the earth). Do not do anything to it; be still and wait. If we try to hurt it, may be it will ride into that hill again, or may be something bad will happen. Let us wait.'

"As it drew nearer, they could see that it was a man coming, and that he was on some strange animal. The Piegans wanted their chief to go toward him and speak to him. The chief did not wish to do this; he was afraid; but at last he started to go to meet the Kutenai, who was coming. When he got near to him, the Kutenai made signs that he was friendly, and patted his horse on his neck and made signs to the chief. 'I give you this animal.' The chief made signs that he was friendly, and the Kutenais rode into the camp and were received as friends, and food was given them and they ate, and their hunger was satisfied.

"The Kutenai stayed with these Piegans for some time, and the Kutenai man told the chief that he had more horses at his camp up in the mountains, and that beyond the mountains there were plenty of horses. The Piegan said, 'I have never heard of a man riding an animal like this.' He asked the Kutenai to bring in the rest of his horses; and one night he started out, and the next day came back driving all his horses before him, and they came to the camp, and all the people saw them and looked at them and wondered.

"Some time after this the Kutenai said to the Piegan chief: 'My friend, why not come across the mountains to my country and visit me? I should like to have you see my country. Bring with you those of your people who wish to come. My people will give you many horses.'

"Then the Piegan chief said: 'It is good. I will go with you and visit you.' He told his people that he was going with this Kutenai, and that any of them who wished to do so might go with him. Many of the Piegans packed their dogs with their lodges and with dried meat and started with the Kutenai, and those who had no dogs packed dried meat in their parfleches and carried it on their backs.

"In those days the Piegans did not take women to sit beside them until they were near middle life—about thirty-five or forty years old; but among those who went across the mountains was a young man less than thirty years old, who had taken a wife. Many of the people did not like this, and some made fun of him because he had taken a wife so young.

"The party had not travelled many days when they got across the mountains, and near to where the Kutenai camp was. When they had come near it, the Kutenai man went on ahead, and when he had reached his village, he told the chief that he had with him visitors, Piegans who lived on the prairie, and that they had no horses, but had plenty of buffalo meat. The Kutenai chief told the man to bring these Piegans into the camp. He did so, and they were well received and were given presents of horses, and they traded their buffalo meat for more horses. The young man with the wife had four parfleches of dried meat, and for each one of these he received a horse, and all four were mares.

"The Piegans stayed with the Kutenais a long time, but at length they returned over the mountains to their own country, taking their horses with them. When the other bands of the Piegans saw these horses and heard what had happened, they began to make peace with the Kutenais, and to trade with them for more horses. The young man who had a wife kept the four mares, and took them about with him wherever he went. He said to his wife: "We will not give away any of these horses. They are all mares and all young. They will breed and soon we will have more.' The mares bred, and the young man, as he grew older, proved to be a good warrior. He began to go to war against the Snakes, and to take horses from them, and after a time he had a great herd of horses.

"This young man, though once everybody had laughed at him, finally became head chief of the Piegans. His name at first was Dog, and afterward Sits in the Middle, and at last Many Horses. He had so many horses he could not keep track of them all. After he had so many horses, he would select ten boys out of each band of the Piegans to care for his horses. Many Horses had more horses than all the rest of the tribe. Many Horses died a good many years ago. These were the first horses the Piegans saw.

"When they first got horses the people did not know what they fed on. They would offer the animals pieces of dried meat, or would take a piece of backfat and rub their noses with it, to try to get them to eat it. Then the horses would turn away and put down their heads, and begin to eat the grass of the prairie."

The date first mentioned by Wolf Calf would be —if we assume his age to be given correctly—about 1804–1806, or when he was from ten to twelve years of age, and I presume that their first horses may have come into the hands of the Blackfeet about that time, or in the very earliest years of the present century. This would agree fairly well with the statement of Mr. Hugh Monroe, who says that in 1813, when he first came among this people, they had possessed horses for a short time only, and had recently begun to make war excursions to the south on a large scale for the purpose of securing more horses from their enemies. Hugh Monroe's wife, who was born about 1796–1798, used to say that when she was a little girl the Piegans had no horses, dogs being their only beasts of burden, and all the evidence that I can gather in this tribe seems to point to the date given as that at which they obtained their first horses. We know that the chief Many Horses was killed in the great battle of the Cypress Hills in the autumn of 1867, and he is always spoken of as a very old man at that time.

Wolf Calf also gave the following account of the first visit of white traders to a Piegan camp. He said: "White people had begun to come into this country, and Many Horses' young men wanted ropes and iron arrowpoints and saddle blankets, and the people were beginning to kill furs and skins to trade. Many Horses began to trade with his own people for these things. He would ask the young men of the tribe to kill skins for him, and they would bring them to him and he would give them a horse or two in exchange. Then he would send his relations in to the Hudson

Bay post to trade, but he would never go himself. The white men wanted to see him, and sent word to him to come in, but he would never do so.

"At length, one winter, these white men packed their dog sledges with goods and started to see Many Horses. They took with them guns. The Piegans heard that the whites were coming, and Many Horses sent word to all the people to come together and meet him at a certain place, where the whites were coming. When these came to the camp, they asked where Many Horses' lodge was, and the people pointed out to them the Crow painted lodge. The whites went to this lodge and began to unpack their things—guns, clothing, knives, and goods of all kinds.

"Many Horses sent two men to go in different directions through the camp and ask all the principal men, young and old, to come together to his lodge. They all came. Some went in and some sat outside. Then these white men began to distribute the guns, and with each gun they gave a bundle of powder and ball. At this same time, the young men received white blankets and the old men black coats. Then we first got knives, and the white men showed us how to use knives; to split down the legs and rip up the belly—to skin for trade. There were not knives enough for each to have one, and it was then that knives with tin edges were made.

"The whites showed us many things. They had flint, steel, and punk, and showed the Indians how to use them. A white man held the flint and struck it with the steel and lighted the punk. Then he gave them to an Indian and told him to do the same. He did so, but when he saw the spark burning the tinder, he was frightened and dropped it.

"Before that, fire was made with firesticks, the twirling stick, being made of greasewood, was hard, and in the hollow which received the point, finely powdered dry grass was put, which caught the fire. This was transferred to tinder and blown into a flame."

As I have said elsewhere, the possession of guns and horses transformed the Blackfeet from a more or less stationary people dwelling in the timber, and devoting all their energies to hunting and the food supply, to a tribe whose chief ambition was the acquiring of glory and riches by warlike pursuits. Now they began to go to war, and in a few years they had conquered from their enemies on the south a great territory, and had begun to make themselves rich in horses. Inhabiting a country abounding in buffalo, it was easy for them to procure robes to supply to the traders who at length penetrated their country, and so to provide themselves with all the goods that the white men offered. But fast in the wake of the white men followed disease, and smallpox and measles and scarlet fever breaking out in their camps, swept off thousands upon thousands of the race. The white men learned that Indians liked liquor and began to use this in trade, and liquor killed more than disease.

Any tribe of Indians who had obtained possessions of any sort from the white men had manifestly a tremendous advantage over any other tribe who still had only their primitive equipment, and we are told by Cheyenne tradition that that brave and warlike people during their migration toward the southwest were utterly routed and put to flight by the Assiniboines, who had recently obtained guns from the white traders.

As a rule, the early intercourse between Indians

and whites in the west was friendly, and their relations pleasant. Yet among the more warlike tribes, stranger and enemy were synonymous terms, so that the horses of white men were often stolen. Of course, when this occurred, efforts were made to kill the thieves, and thus active war was very often brought about. A man or two killed on either side would for some time to come insure reprisals and fighting at all subsequent meetings of parties of whites and Indians belonging to the tribe engaged, and each battle would make others more probable. Sometimes a peace would be made which was lasting, and there are some tribes which have never engaged in any wars with the whites, while others, in the face of shameful injury and ill treatment, have always been their faithful allies in their wars with other tribes.

APPENDIX.

THE Indians of this continent constitute a single race, whose physical characteristics are remarkably alike throughout all tribes. Though the diverse conditions of life in various parts of a wide continent have caused differences of stature, colour, and development in certain directions, these differences are of minor importance, and it is probable that there is no such wide variation as is found among different groups of the white, black, and yellow races.

An Indian is always an Indian, yet each tribe has its own characteristics. The popular notion that all Indians have the same speech and the same modes of life is wholly erroneous. In North America, north of Mexico, there were nearly sixty distinct linguistic stocks or groups of languages, which, so far as known, had no relation to each other, and represent groups of Indians apparently unconnected by ties of blood with any other family. In other words, these tribes differ from each other in speech more widely than do the different European nations; for all the European nations, such as Russian, German, Italian—except the intrusive Turks, Huns, etc.—constitute parts of a single linguistic stock, the Indo-European or Aryan. The difference between two Indian linguistic stocks, such as Algonquin and Dakota, is, therefore, not that between Greeks and Germans, but between the greater groups Aryan and Turanian, or Aryan and Semetic, and such stocks as Algonquin, Dakota, Pawnee, Athabascan, and Iroquois constitute families of equal relative rank with the Old World families just mentioned.

While some of the Indian families were made up of many tribes speaking different dialects, or even using languages unintelligible to each other, and controlling a vast extent of territory, others consisted of a single small tribe without apparent affinities with any of its neighbours. So, on the Pacific coast, where about two thirds of the different linguistic stocks exist, one may find a little village of fishing Indians who —they say—have from time immemorial inhabited this same region, and who yet have nothing in common with their nearest neighbours a few miles away, and are unable to communicate with them except by signs, or —to-day—by the so-called Chinook jargon, the common trade language of the northwest coast.

But while a vast territory might be inhabited and controlled by one family, as much of the eastern United States and Canada nearly as far as the Rocky Mountains was controlled by the Algonquin family, this occupancy did not necessarily mean that all other families were excluded from such territory. At various points all over such a region, there might be areas, large or small, which were held by tribes genetically distinct from the prevailing family and holding their own against their neighbours.

As the families differed from each other in language, so the tribes differed in culture. North of the Mexican boundary, all tribes were practically in the

stone age of development. The use of metals was unknown. In a few cases, native copper was employed
for ornament or utensil, but it was treated as a stone—
hammered into shape. It was not known as a metal.
The Indian's arms were made of stone, chipped, hammered, and ground from flint or some other hard rock.
His clothing was made of skin. Many tribes made
pottery of a very simple kind, useful for dishes and
cooking utensils. Their permanent dwellings were as
varied as the regions which they inhabited, yet in their
movable lodges or tipis, which were made of skins or
bark, one type prevailed over almost the whole continent. While the subsistence of the people was largely
derived from hunting and fishing, or from the wild
fruits of the earth, yet a very large proportion of the
tribes practised agriculture. This is especially true of
those which inhabited the country of abundant rainfall lying between the Atlantic Ocean and the Mississippi River, yet it was by no means confined to these
alone, for many tribes of the high dry plains, of Pawnee, Dakota, and, in ancient times, Algonquin stock,
raised crops of corn, beans, and squashes. The tribes
of the extreme southwest depended for support very
largely on agriculture, and practised irrigation.

Picture writings were used among almost all the
tribes, but were, of course, carried to their greatest
perfection among those families whose culture was
highest. Among the Nahuatl and Mayas of the south,
and the Algonquins and Iroquois of the north, such
picture writings—on skin, bark, or cloth—sometimes
took the form of long historical documents, or served
to render permanent the ritual of important ceremonies. But even among the nomads of the plains,
paintings on skins often commemorated the important

17

events of the year, sometimes by months, and some of these ran back for many years—even, it is said, for a century. Such writings were, if not history, at least records.

The social condition of the North Americans has been greatly misunderstood. The place of woman in the tribe was not that of a slave or of a beast of burden. The existence of the gentile organization, in most tribes with descent in the female line, forbade any such subjugation of woman. In many tribes women took part in the councils of the chiefs; in some, women were even the tribal rulers; while in all they received a fair measure of respect and affection from those related to them. At a council held in 1791 with the Huron-Iroquois the women spoke to the American commissioner as follows: "You ought to hear and listen to what we women shall speak as well as the sachems, for we are the owners of this land, and it is ours. It is we that plant it for our and their use. Hear us, therefore, for we speak of things that concern us and our children."

Among the Mokis and other Pueblos, and among the Navajoes, men and women work together in the fields. With the Mokis the young unmarried women are not expected or allowed to perform such heavy work as carrying water up the mesa, and with the Navajoes a man may even cut out and sew a buckskin shirt. Just at present, the keeper of the tribal medicine of the Kiowas is a woman, and in the same tribe the grandmother practically rules the family, although she works as hard as the other women. Among the Cheyennes the woman has great influence.

The notion that women were slaves no doubt had its origin in the fact that their duties are such as civilized men commonly regard as toil, while the more arduous pursuits of hunting and war are looked upon by white men as amusements. As a matter of fact, the labours of this savage life were not unevenly divided between the sexes. In their home life the Indians were much like other people. The men, as a rule, were affectionate husbands and fathers, often undergoing severe sacrifices and privations for the sake of their families. Parents were devotedly attached to their children, and a strong feeling existed between the members of a family, even though the tie of blood uniting them was remote.

Another misconception of Indian character has obtained a firm footing in the popular mind. It is generally believed that these people are grave, taciturn, and sullen in their ordinary life. This is far from being true. Instead, they are fond of society, gossipy, great talkers, with a keen sense of humour and great quickness of repartee. In their villages and their camps, frequent visits were paid from lodge to lodge. In time of plenty, feasts were continual, and social gatherings for dancing, story-telling, or conversation occurred more often than in civilized communities. Constantly among young men, and often among young women, were formed friendships which remind one of the attachment that existed between David and Jonathan, and such friendships frequently lasted through life, or were interrupted only when family ties were assumed.

It is in the system of government devised by some of them that the North Americans show their greatest advance in culture. The so-called civilizations of the south—of Peru and Mexico—while much higher than those of tribes inhabiting the territory now the United

States and Canada, yet differed from them in degree rather than in kind, and the league of the Iroquois, since it has been thoroughly understood, has challenged admiration both for its organization and its purposes. This was an offensive and defensive federation of five tribes—the Onondagas, Oneidas, Senecas, Cayugas, and Mohawks—formed by the Onondaga chief Hiawatha about the middle of the sixteenth century. Of it Mr. Hale says: "The system he devised was to be not a loose and transitory league but a permanent government. While each nation was to retain its own council and management of local affairs, the general control was to be lodged in a federal senate, composed of representatives to be elected by each nation, holding office during good behaviour, and acknowledged as ruling chiefs throughout the whole confederacy. Still further and more remarkable, the federation was not to be a limited one. It was to be indefinitely expansible. The avowed design of its purpose was to abolish war altogether." As is well said by Dr. Brinton, "Certainly this scheme was one of the most farsighted, and in its aim beneficent, which any statesman has ever designed for man."

As a rule, the government of the Indians was a simple democracy. The chiefs were usually elected—though sometimes hereditary—and held office for life, or until advancing years caused their resignation. As has been said, women were sometimes made chiefs. Often the chief of a tribe was chosen from the chiefs of the gentes by his fellow chiefs. In one of the tribes of the Iroquois league the council which elected the chief was composed altogether of women. But the chief's power was not absolute. In minor matters which pertained to the ordinary affairs of the everyday life of the people, he acted independently and his orders were obeyed, but grave concerns, such as quarrels between prominent men, relations with neighbouring tribes, the making of war or peace, were discussed in a council of chiefs and prominent men, where each individual was at liberty to express his opinion and to cast his vote. The head chief acted as the presiding officer of such council, and if he was a strong man his views carried great weight; but unless he could win over to his side a majority of the council he had to yield. Thus the chief's authority was personal rather than official, but for this very reason it was strong; for, where the office was elective, that man was made chief who had proved by his deeds from childhood to middle age that he was a more able man than his fellows—that he was brave in war, wise in peace, careful for the well-being of his people in the everyday affairs of life, generous and kindly, yet firm—in short, that he was a leader in time of war and a father in time of peace. His council was composed of men young and old, some one of whom might later take his place.

I give a brief sketch of the past and present homes and conditions of some of the more important of the North American family stocks.

ALGONQUIN.

The area occupied by this family was far more extensive than that held by any other North American stock. On the Atlantic seaboard they controlled the territory from Labrador on the north to North Carolina on the south. From Labrador westward, tribes of this stock occupied all of British America nearly to the Rocky Mountains and south of Peace River and

Churchill River. They also held parts of what are now North Dakota, Minnesota, Wisconsin, Iowa, and Missouri, all of Illinois, Indiana, Kentucky, and West Virginia, and most of Michigan, Ohio, and Maryland. There was a settlement in South Carolina, and a western branch had pushed its way into South Dakota and Wyoming, and westward into Colorado. No other family of North Americans held territory at all comparable for extent or for excellence—either in fertility or abundance of game—with that possessed by the Algonquins, who, in numbers, intelligence, and physical qualities, stand among the first of the families of North American Indians.

It is impossible to conjecture what were the numbers of the Algonquins before the coming of the whites, but we may imagine that they were large. If the territory which they inhabited was thinly settled, it was also vast. Most of the southeastern tribes of this stock practised agriculture as well as hunting, and inhabiting as they did a fertile country, which also abounded in game and in natural fruits, it may be conjectured that they found little or no difficulty in supporting life. It is not likely that in primitive times they often suffered from hunger. They were brave, too, and well able to defend themselves against the attacks of their enemies, and there would seem to be no reason why this naturally vigorous stock should not have been very numerous, at least until it approached the point where the food question became troublesome.

In the vast territory occupied by the Algonquins there were many different tribes, and it is not to be imagined that all of these recognised the tie of blood which connected them, or that all of this family were necessarily friends and allies. The reverse of this was true, and quarrels and wars between different tribes probably took place frequently. Yet often the tribes of this blood united against the fierce Iroquois, whose territory about the easternmost of the Great Lakes and the upper St. Lawrence River, lay in the very midst of the Algonquin lands, and another division of which bordered these lands upon the south. Between these two great families there was a deep and bitter hostility, sometimes interrupted by intervals of peace, which, however, were not of long duration. To this rule the Wyandots, descendants of the old Hurons, were a notable exception. They were uniformly allies of the Algonquins.

The date at which the westernmost branches of the Algonquin stock came to their present homes is comparatively recent, for it is within the last two hundred and fifty years that the Arapahoes—including the Gros Ventres of the prairie—the Blackfeet, and the Cheyennes reached the Continental Divide. If we may believe Cheyenne tradition, they were the first tribe to penetrate as far as the Rocky Mountains. Their oral history tells that with the Arapahoes they came into the Black Hills country, in Dakota, about two hundred and twenty-five years ago, having journeyed from the northeast, perhaps originally from the shores of Lake Superior, or possibly of Hudson Bay, for they describe an immense body of water in a barren, treeless country, abounding in great rocks. The Blackfeet came next. They say that not many generations ago they lived near Peace River, far from the mountains. To the east of them were the timber Crees, and to the north tribes of Athabascan stock. They made their way slowly south and west, and probably reached the Rocky Mountains less than one hundred and fifty years ago.

The following list of the principal tribes of the Algonquin stock is taken in part from Brinton and from Powell:

ABNAKI = "eastlanders." Nova Scotia and south bank of the St. Lawrence River.

ALGONQUIN = people living "on the other side" of the stream. North of the St. Lawrence River, Ontario, and Quebec.

ARAPAHOE = "traders"(?) (Dunbar). Flanks of the Rocky Mountains from Black Hills to head waters of the Arkansas River.

BLACKFOOT. Flanks of the Rocky Mountains from the Saskatchewan River south to Yellowstone River.

CHEYENNE = "red or painted"—i. e., alien, so-called by the Sioux (Clark). Flanks of the Rocky Mountains from Black Hills to head waters of Arkansas River.

CREE, abbreviated from Kiristinon = "killer"(?). Southern and western shores of Hudson Bay, west to Rocky Mountains.

DELAWARE, or Leni Lenapi = "original, or principal, men." Along the Delaware River.

ILLINOIS, from ilini = "men." On the Illinois River.

KICKAPOO = people of the river, "easily navigable." Upper Illinois River.

MAHICAN, a dialectic form of Mohegan, but a distinct tribe. Lower Hudson River.

MIAMI = "pigeon." Miami and Upper Wabash Rivers.

MIKMAK. Nova Scotia.

MILISIT = "broken talkers." New Brunswick.

MENOMINI = "wild rice people." About Green Bay, Wisconsin.

MOHEGAN. Lower Connecticut River.

MONTAGNAIS = "mountaineers" (French writers). Northern shores of lower St. Lawrence River.

MASSACHUSETT = people "at the Blue Hills." On Massachusetts Bay.

MONTAUK = people at the "manito tree." Eastern Long Island.

NANTICOKE. Eastern shore of Chesapeake Bay.

OJIBWA or CHIPPEWA = people of the "puckered moccasin"(?) (Warren). Ontario River.

PANTICO. North of Pamlico Sound.

PIANKASHA = "western people." On lower Wabash River.

POTTAWATOMI = "blowers"—i. e., "council firemakers." South of Lake Michigan.

SAC(Fox) = "yellow earth" people (Drake). About Rock River, Illinois.

SHAWANO or SHAWNEE = southern people. On Cumberland River.

Most of the eastern tribes of the Algonquins have long been extinct, having either perished utterly, or their scattered fragments having migrated and joined other tribes, in which they have become merged. But these extinct tribes will not be wholly forgotten, for their names are fixed in the geography of this country, and will thus be preserved so long as America shall endure.

In the Seventh Annual Report of the Bureau of Ethnology, published in 1891, the present number of the Algonquin race is given as ninety-five thousand, of which about sixty thousand are in Canada and the remainder in the United States. Many of these last are self-supporting and more or less civilized, though still clinging tenaciously to many of their ancient beliefs and practices. The same volume contains a list of the tribes officially recognized, and their present numbers and locations, compiled chiefly from the Report for 1889 of the United States Commissioner of Indian Affairs and the Canadian Report for 1888, which gives the following facts:

ABNAKI, including Passamaquoddies and Milisits in Maine, New Brunswick, and Quebec. 1,874(?).

ALGONQUIN, in Ontario and Quebec, Canada. 4,767(?).

ARAPAHOE, at Cheyenne agency, Oklahoma Territory, and at Shoshoni agency, Wyoming. 2,157.

The Atse'na or Gros Ventres of the Prairie, a detached band of the Arapahoes, are not mentioned in this list. They are at the Fort Belknap agency in northern Montana with the Assiniboines, and number about 509.

BLACKFOOT, at the Blackfoot agency, Montana, at Calgary, and on Belly River, in Northwest Territories, 6,743.

CHEYENNE, at Cheyenne agency, Oklahoma Territory, Tongue River agency, Montana, and Pine Ridge agency, South Dakota, 3,473.

CREE, in Manitoba and the Northwest Territories. A few Crees who were engaged in the Riel rebellion took refuge in Montana, where they still remain, supporting themselves by trapping and the sale of articles which they manufacture. 17,386.

DELAWARE, about one thousand are incorporated and live with the Cherokees in the Indian Territory, others are with the Wichitas in the Indian Territory, the Senecas and Onondagas in New York, the Chippewas on the Thames River in Ontario, the Six Nations on Grand River, Ontario, and with the Chippewas at the Pottawatomi agency in Kansas. 1,750 (?).

KICKAPOO—a part are at the Sac and Fox agency, Indian Territory, others at the Pottawatomi agency, Kansas, and some in Mexico. 762(?).

MENOMINI, at Green Bay agency, Wisconsin. 1,311.

MIAMI, Quapaw agency, Indian Territory, and in Indiana. 374 (?).

MICMAC, in Nova Scotia, New Brunswick, Prince Edward Island, and Quebec, Canada. 4,108.

MISSISAUGA, with Monsoni, Muskegon, etc., in Ontario and Rupert's Land, Canada. 4,790.

MONTAGANIS, Quebec. 1,919.

NASCOAPEE, Quebec. 2,860.

OJIBWA or CHIPPEWA, at White Earth agency, Minnesota; La Pointe agency, Wisconsin; Mackina agency, Michigan; Devil's Lake agency, North Dakota; Pottawatomi agency, Kansas; Chippewas of Lake Superior, Lake Huron, Sarnia, on the Thames, on Walpole Island, on Manitoulin and Cockburn Islands, all in Ontario, Canada, and Sauteux and Chippewas in Manitoba. 31,928(?).

OTTAWA, at Quapaw agency, Indian Territory; at Mackina agency, Michigan; on Manitoulin and Cockburn Islands, Ontario, Canada. 4,794(?).

PEORIA, Quapaw agency, Indian Territory. 160.

POTTAWATOMI, at the Sac and Fox agency, Oklahoma Territory; Pottawatomi agency, Kansas; Mackina agency, Michigan; Prairie Band, Wisconsin; on Walpole Island, Ontario, Canada. 1,465.

SAC and Fox, at Sac and Fox agency, Oklahoma Territory; Sac and Fox agency, Iowa; Pottawatomi agency, Kansas. 973.

SHAWNEE, Quapaw agency, Indian Territory; Sac and Fox agency, Oklahoma Territory; incorporated with the Cherokees, Indian Territory. 1,519.

STOCKBRIDGE (Mohican), at Green Bay. Wisconsin, and in New York with The Tuscaroras   and Senecas. 117.

ATHABASCAN.

What the Algonquin linguistic family was to eastern North America the Athabascan was to the west. Both touched the land of the Innuit on the north, and the east and west range of each covered sixty degrees of longitude, so that between Hudson Bay and the Rocky Mountains the countries of the two overlapped; but while the southernmost tribe of the Algonquin was only thirty degrees from the northern limit of the family, at least forty degrees of latitude separated the Athabascans of the Arctic from those of Mexico. This great north and south area was, however, not continuous. There was a wide territory, extending over fourteen or fifteen degrees of latitude, where—except for a few small settlements on the Pacific coast—no Athabascans were found.

Although the area occupied by the Athabascans was so extensive, it presented in its adaptability for human occupancy a marked contrast to that possessed by the Algonquins. These, in their southern territory, inhabited a country of abundant rainfall, fertile and admirably adapted for agricultural pursuits, while those Athabascans who were not dwellers in the frozen north occupied an arid, desert country, where rains are infrequent and agriculture impossible, except by means of irrigation.

Physically, the members of this family are moderately well developed, being often tall and muscular and very enduring, but those of the north are said to be short-lived. They are a strong and masterful people, and Mr. Mooney, who has seen much of them, writes me: "Excepting in the extreme north we find the Tinne tribes almost everywhere asserting and exercising superiority over their neighbours. This applies to the detached bands in Washington, Oregon, and California, and to the Navajoes in the south. The Tinne tribes in California have imposed their language and tribal regulations upon their neighbours. The Navajoes are pre-eminent stock raisers, weavers, and metal workers. The Apache are our wiliest Indian fighters, and were steadily driving the civilized Mexicans southward, when the United States interfered."

As might be supposed from the distance which separates the homes of the northern and southern groups of this family, the two differed widely in their ways and modes of life. The Athabascans of the north were hunters and fishermen. In summer they followed the great game or spread their nets in the lakes; in winter they harnessed their dogs to the sledges and careered over the frozen wastes. The desert-inhabiting Apaches and Navajoes of the south know neither dog sledges nor boats. They are mountaineers and hunters, famed for their endurance and able to take

Navajo Weaver

up the track of a deer, and between sunrise and sunset to run him down and kill him with a knife. Although hunters, they are also tillers of the soil, raising corn and other vegetables, and gathering the nuts of the piñon, the bean of the mesquite, and the root of the American aloe.

The Athabascans use lodges of skin or bark in the north, and in the south rude huts made of branches of trees. They make pottery and wickerwork baskets, which are so tightly woven that they serve as water vessels, and their stone metates used for grinding corn are far more efficient implements than the mortar in which the grain was pounded by tribes further to the east. The canoes of the interior tribes of the north are of bark. The Navajoes have long been renowned for the handsome blankets which they weave. This with them is not an aboriginal art, but is borrowed from their immediate neighbours the Mokis and Zuñis, with whom and with some northwest coast tribes it is aboriginal, for the latter weave excellent blankets from the fleece of the wild white goat.

Among the tribes of this family, great differences exist in the gentile systems and in the laws of consanguinity. In some tribes, descent is in the female line, and a man considers his father no relation, while in other tribes the son belongs to his father's gens.

Of the northern group of the Athabascans, the southernmost tribe inhabiting the central region are the Sarsi, who for many years have lived with the Blackfeet. These are an offshoot of the Beaver Indians, and, according to tradition, left their own country about one hundred years ago on account of a quarrel with another camp of their own people, and migrated southward. They joined the Blackfeet, and have lived with them ever since.

Among the best-known tribes of Athabascan stock are the

APACHE = "enemies." Arizona and Northern Mexico.

ATNA = "strangers." On Copper River, Alaska.

BEAVER. On Peace River, British America.

CHIPPEWYAN = "pointed coats." Coast of Hudson Bay and north of Crees.

HUPA. California, Trinity River.

KENAI = "people." Kenai Peninsula, Alaska.

KUCHIN = "people." Yukon River, Alaska.

NAVAJO = "whetstone or knife-whetting people" (Mooney). New Mexico and Arizona.

NEHANI = "yellow knives" (?). Upper Stikine River, Alaska.

SARSI. Beaver offshoot.

SIKANI. Upper Peace River, British America.

SLAVE. Upper Mackenzie River, British America.

TAKULI = "carriers." Fraser River, British Columbia.

TUTUTENA. Rogue River, Oregon.

UMPQUA. Near Salem, Oregon.

WAILAKI = people of the "northern language." Northern California.

The northern tribes of this group are more generally known as Hare Indians, Dog Ribs, Chippewyans, Yellow Knives (Nehani), Strong Bows, Carrier (Takuli), etc. There are supposed to be about thirty-three thousand Athabascans, of whom about one fourth belong to the northern group. Of the southern tribes the best known are the various bands of Apaches inhabiting Arizona and Mexico, who have shown themselves so fierce in war and so apt in escaping the troops sent in pursuit of them, and the Navajoes, whose fame rests in large measure on the peaceful art of blanket weaving. The Apaches are still more or less wild, and have not made very great progress toward civilization; but the Navajoes possess some cattle, many horses, and great herds of sheep and goats, and have long been self-supporting. They are well-disposed and industrious, saving and progressive, and in advancement toward civilization stand high among the tribes of the west. They probably number between eighteen and twenty thousand.

The small tribes of Athabascans of the Pacific coast are at various agencies in California and Oregon, usually with tribes of other stocks. They are moderately advanced, till the ground, raise some live stock, and the men labour for the whites in the salmon canneries, the hop fields, and on the farms.

DAKOTA.

Six States of the Union bear the names of tribes of the Dakota stock, and of late years no group of North American Indians has been better known than these. At the time when general immigration to the country west of the Mississippi began, this family occupied much of the territory entered on by the whites, and for a number of years conflicts and wars were frequent, culminating in 1876 with the Custer battle. For a few years after that, the army was at work clearing out the scattered camps of hostile Sioux in Montana and Dakota, but since that time there has been nothing in the nature of a general war between this stock and the whites, though there was a short-lived but bloody outbreak in 1890–'91.

The name Dakota or Lahkota, by which the principal tribes of this stock, the Sioux, call themselves, means "confederated," "allied," while the commoner term Sioux is a French corruption of an Algonquin word, *nadowe' si-ug,* meaning originally "snakes," and so enemies. In this sense it has been used by the Ojibwa in modern times, although not as applied to the Sioux.

History and tradition find several of the most important tribes of the Dakotas occupying upper Michigan, Wisconsin, and eastern Minnesota, though long before this some must have taken the journey to and across the Great Plains. The Crows have occupied the eastern flanks of the Rocky Mountains, and the Stonies—a tribe of the Assiniboines—the mountains still further north for a very long time. The Assiniboines, too, must long have lived in the prairie country of what is now eastern North Dakota, for—according to Cheyenne tradition—they were there when these last migrated from the northeast. It is probable, however, that the great body of those tribes now known in the vernacular as Sioux, lived in early historic times about the western great lakes and the head waters of the Mississippi. From this territory they were driven, or crowded out, by the westward movement of the Algonquin tribes and by settlements, and spread themselves over much of the Great Plains.

An eastern origin is now pretty well established for this stock, for in Virginia, North and South Carolina, and Mississippi were the homes of tribes now extinct, which philologists class with this stock.* Such were the Catawba in South Carolina; the Tutelo, Saponi, and Woccon, in North Carolina; the Occaneechi in Virginia; the Biloxi and possibly other tribes in Mississippi. Catlin has shown that the Mandans reached the Missouri River by travelling down the Ohio. With-

---

*Mooney, The Siouan Tribes of the East, Bulletin Bureau of Ethnology, Washington.

in recent times a number of the Dakota tribes have occupied the timbered country, and have not been dwellers on the plains. Such are the Winnebagoes, Osages, Quapaws, Missourias, and others.

Physically and intellectually the Dakotas stand high, and in stature and development the mountain Crows are exceeded by no tribe in the west, unless it be the Cheyennes and Arapahoes.

Most of the tribes have lost the agricultural habits which all probably once possessed, and which the Mandans, Hidatsa, and some others still practise. Others have only recently given up this habit, as occasionally shown by a sub-tribal name—as Mini-co-o-ju—"They plant by the water." Some of the Dakotas manufactured pottery, and the Mandans even made blue glass beads—after the coming of the whites. This tribe, too, occupied permanent houses.

There was the widest variation in the gentile system, where it existed at all. With some, descent was in the male, with others, in the female line. The chieftainship was hereditary, descending from father to son, though an early traveller found the Winnebagoes ruled over by a woman chief. The country held by the Dakota stock in modern times included a part of Wisconsin and of western Minnesota, most of North Dakota, Iowa, and Missouri, more than half of Arkansas, Montana, and Wyoming, South Dakota, and a large part of eastern Nebraska and Kansas, and parts of British America near the Rocky Mountains. Within the last hundred years their neighbours have been, on the north and east and a part of the west, Algonquins; on the south Pawnees, Shoshonis, and Kiowas; and on the west, Shoshonis, Kiowas, and Algonquins. Besides this, their territory was interrupted by settlements of Pawnees, who, having invaded their territory, had driven out, conquered, or were still at war with various tribes of this stock.

Most of the plains tribes of Dakota stock depended for food upon the buffalo and were wanderers, following the herds from place to place, and, on the prairie, dwelling in the conical skin lodges, which were the common habitations of the plains tribes.

The principal tribes of the Dakota stock are:

ABSORAKA = "Crows" (?). (The name seems to refer to some kind of bird.)

ASSINIBOINES = "stone boilers." On Saskatchewan, Souris, and Assiniboine River, British America.

BILOXI. Biloxi Bay, Mississippi.

CATAWBA. Catawba River, South Carolina.

CROWS (or Absoraka). On Yellowstone River, North Dakota.

DAKOTA PROPER or SIOUX = "confederate." Western Minnesota, North and South Dakota.

IOWA = "sleepy ones." On the Iowa River, Iowa.

KANSA or KAW. On the Kansas River, Kansas.

MANDAN. Upper Missouri River, North Dakota.

HIDATSA or MINITARIS, a branch of the Crows = "those who cross the water" (Minitari). Upper Missouri River, North Dakota.

MISSOURIA = people of the Great Muddy. Originally on lower Missouri River, Missouri

OCCANEECHI. Southern Virginia.

OMAHA = "upper stream people." Niobrara River, Nebraska,

OSAGE. In southern Missouri.

OTO. On lower Platte River, Nebraska.

PONCA. Northwestern Nebraska.

QUAPAW or ARKANSA, "down stream people," On the lower Arkansas, Arkansas.

SAPONI. Central North Carolina.

WINNEBAGO = "stinking lake people." Eastern Wisconsin.

The number of people of the Dakota stock is estimated to be about 45,000, and of these about 42,000

Group of Assiniboines

are in the United States. About 24,000 belong to the Sioux tribes, as the term is commonly applied, 1,700 to the Assiniboines, 1,200 to the Omahas, 1,600 to the Osages, 2,200 to the Winnebagoes, and 3,000 to the Crows, including the Minitaris or Hidatsa. Most of these Indians have made considerable progress toward civilization. They have cattle, cultivate the ground with some success, and, as a rule, live in log houses. There are no longer any "wild" Indians among them, and they are becoming—though slowly—a fairly hard-working part of the population of the West. Their various reservations and agencies, of which there are many, are situated in Wisconsin, Minnesota, the Dakotas, Montana, Nebraska, Kansas, and the Indian Territory.

IROQUOIS.

In the early history of America no Indian family was better known than the Iroquois—a name given to a group of tribes, some of whom made up the celebrated Six Nations. The territory occupied by this family lay wholly in the east, and in two principal situations. The northernmost of these included territory on both sides of the St. Lawrence River, from where Quebec now stands, westward to Lake Huron, all about Lakes Ontario and Erie, and south to the Chesapeake Bay. They thus held portions of Canada, Ohio, Michigan, Central New York, and the greater part of Pennsylvania, southward along the valley of the Susquehanna to the salt water. The other Iroquois were established almost in one body in Virginia, Tennessee, North and South Carolina, Georgia, and Alabama. The northern territory was surrounded on all sides by lands occupied by the Algonquins, while the southern group of the tribes had for neighbours Algonquins on the north and west, Dakotas on the east, and Muskogis on the south.

No Indian family excelled the Iroquois in physical development or in culture. The records of the civil war, in which some companies of Iroquois fought, show that these stood highest of any bodies of our soldiers in stature and in physical strength and vigour. Intellectually they ranked as high. The league of the five nations—Cayugas, Mohawks, Oneidas, Onondagas, and Senecas—to which was afterward added a sixth, the Tuscaroras, alone stamps them as a stock whose intellectual vigour exceeded that of their neighbours. Their intelligence was shown in other ways. They were, to a greater extent than almost any other Indian family, agriculturists, and their crops supplied each year more food than they could possibly consume. They lived in permanent villages, but in most other respects their everyday life was not markedly different from that of other Indians.

It was among the Iroquois that the gentile system obtained its highest development among our northern tribes. Descent was in the 'female line, and mothers in the Iroquois villages had a power and an influence greater than those of the men. They were the owners of the land and of most of the personal property; they were the councillors of the tribes, and sometimes even its chiefs. The ancient gentile system of these people still persists, even among the civilized Iroquois, on their reservations in Central New York, and on Grand River, Ontario, and of late years this has become a cause of more or less heartburning and dissatisfaction. Among the Senecas to-day half-breed children of an Indian father and a white woman are called by

the Senecas whites, are not allowed to draw tribal an-
nuities, nor to have any share in the public affairs of
the nation; while the children of a white father and
an Indian mother are regarded as Indians, and have
all an Indian's rights and privileges. The same rule
holds in marriages between Indians of the different
tribes, the child belonging to the tribe of the mother
and not to that of the father. This matter has several
times come up in the courts for adjudication.

The southern group of the Iroquois included the
Cherokees and the Tuscaroras, the former chiefly in
the mountain region of North Carolina and Tennessee,
and the latter in eastern North Carolina. They did
not differ especially from their northern relations.
Like them, they built connected houses of logs, and
fortified their villages. They were industrious agriculturists and made good pottery. The ancestors of
the Cherokees were quite certainly the builders of
some of the famous mounds in Ohio.

The myths, legends, and sacred rituals of the Iroquois are perhaps better known than those of any other
Indians. To assist in the preservation of these they
used certain aids to memory in the shape of beads or
shells strung on buckskin strings, the combination of
the beads suggesting certain facts and events. The
Book of Rites, edited by Mr. Horatio Hale, is an example of the ritual of this remarkable people. The
Cherokees, likewise, had a great body of ritual recorded in their modern native alphabet. Mr. Mooney has
procured practically all of this—about seven hundred
formulas—and expects to translate it all. A part has
already appeared in his Sacred Formulas of the Cherokees, in the Seventh Annual Report of the Bureau of
Ethnology. There is a mass of similar material still

existing in many, if not in most other tribes, although few of these extended productions have been reduced to writing and translated.

The principal tribes of the Iroquois were these:

CAYUGA = people of the "swampy land." South of Lake Ontario, New York.

CHEROKEE. Mountain region of Carolina, Georgia, and Tennessee.

CONESTOGA = "lodge pole people." Lower Susquehanna River, Pennsylvania, and Maryland.

ERIE = "wild cats." South of Lake Erie, Ohio, and New York.

NEUTRAL NATION. West of Niagara River, Ontario.

NOTTAWA = "snake," i. e., enemy. Southern Virginia.

ONEIDA = people of the "stone." Central New York.

ONONDAGA = people of the "little hill." Central New York.

SENECA. Western New York.

TUSCARORA = flax or hemp pullers(?) (Hewitt; Morgan makes it "shirt weavers"). The name refers to a vegetable cloth fibre. Eastern North Carolina.

WYANDOT or HURONS—Huron is the old provincial French for "bear." East of Georgian Bay, Ontario, and south; southwest of Lake Erie in Ohio and Michigan.

The present number of the Iroquois is estimated at about 44,000, of whom about 9,000 are in Canada. The Cherokees—one of the five civilized tribes—make up by far the greater part of these, numbering not far from 28,000, of whom more than 26,000 are in Indian Territory, the remainder forming the eastern band, who are in the counties of Swain, Jackson, Cherokee, and Graham, in North Carolina. The Cherokee nation, however, includes a large number of adopted whites and negroes. Of the Cayugas there are about 1,300, most of them in Canada, but a few in New York and the Indian Territory. About 2,400 Mohawks are in Canada, as are also 1,000 Oneidas, 300 of whom are in New York and 1,700 at Green Bay agency, Wisconsin; 350 Onondagas are in Canada, and 550 on New York reservations. Of the 3,100 Senecas, 127 are at the Quapaw agency, Indian Territory, 200 are in Canada, and the remainder in New York. The Tuscaroras number about 750, of whom about half are in Canada and half in New York. There are 700 Wyandots, 300 at the Quapaw agency and 400 in Canada. Besides these, there are about 4,400 Indians of this stock known as Caughnawagas and St. Regis, in Canada and southern New York, who seem to be a mixture of all the tribes of the Six Nations, the Mohawks predominating. All the Cherokees and all the New York reservation Indians are civilized and self-supporting.

MUSKOGI.

An especial interest attaches to the Muskogi or Chocta-Muskhogi linguistic stock, because its survivors constitute four out of the five so-called civilized tribes, and also because there is a reasonable probability that they are the descendants of some of those people who built the great mounds in the Mississippi Valley and in the Gulf States, which have given rise to so many speculations and theories as to their origin. This stock inhabited the country "from the Savannah River and the Atlantic west to the Mississippi, and from the Gulf of Mexico north to the Tennessee River"; and although the tribes differed somewhat from one another in physical characteristics, their relationship is close.

The culture of this people was high. They were industrious cultivators of the soil, and raised large crops of corn, beans, squashes, and tobacco. Their towns were large and fortified, and often built on high mounds artificially constructed, and their houses substantial, and containing several rooms. Though made of stone, their weapons and utensils were very finely finished.

Their religious system was highly developed and its ritual elaborate, and they had an extensive oral literature. Their mortuary customs were singular, the bodies of the dead in some tribes being exposed until the flesh decayed, when the bones were cleaned and buried in the gentile mound.

The gentile system prevailed, descent being in the female line. Women had a standing equal to that of men, and occasionally one filled the office of chief.

The neighbours of the Muskogi stock were the Algonquins and Iroquois on the north, the Timuquans of Florida, and the isolated Dakota colony of the Biloxi on the south, and the Natches, Tonicas, and southern Dakotas on the west.

Some of the tribes of the Muskogi stock were:

ALIBAMU = "burnt clearing" (*not* "here we rest") (Gatschet). On the Alabama River, Alabama.

APALACHI = "people on the other side" (Gatschet). Apalachi Bay, Florida.

CHAKTA or CHOCTA—from a Spanish word, meaning "flat head" (Gatschet). Southern Mississippi.

CHIKASA or CHICKASAW = "rebels or renegades." Northern Mississippi.

HITCHITI = "looking up ahead" (Gatschet). Southeastern Georgia.

MASKOGI or CREEK PROPER—doubtfully from the Algonquin word *maskigo,* meaning "swampy." Central Alabama.

SEMINOLE = "wanderers or runaways." Northern and Central Florida.

YAMASI = "gentle" (Gatschet). Southern coast of South Carolina.

The territory occupied by this stock is thus seen to be not very large, yet owing to their industrious habits and their adaptability to civilized pursuits, they have made a good struggle for existence, and to-day are doing well and increasing in numbers. The Apalachi and Yamasi are extinct, and but few remain of the Alibamu; but there are 10,000 Choctaws, 2,500 Chickasaws, 9,500 Creeks, and 2,600 Seminoles in the Indian Territory, a few Choctaws in Louisiana, and about 400 Seminoles in Florida. The Indians of this stock who are in the Indian Territory are civilized and well to do.

Besides the stocks already spoken of, there are others, whose importance deserves a more extended mention than can here be given. One of these is the Shoshoni, a family occupying the Rocky Mountains and the plains on the flanks of that range from Red Deer's River—which flows into the Saskatchewan— or perhaps even from the head of Peace River, south through Mexico. This stock includes tribes whose names are well known, and its culture ranged from the lowest to the highest, from the miserable Diggers and Sheep-eaters to the Aztecs, who had some acquaintance with metal, and far exceeded any other North American tribe in their approach to civilization. To this stock belong the brave but peaceful Snakes, the warlike Comanches, the Pai-Utes, the Gosiutes, the mountain-loving Utes, the Mokis, the Guaymas, the Mayas, the Papagos, the Pimas, the Yaquis, the Aztecs, the Tlascalans, and others reaching south to Guatemala. Dr. Brinton gives forty-four tribes of this stock, divided into three groups, and covering territory from British to Central America.

Another family of importance is the Pawnee or Caddo, whose territory extended interruptedly from the Gulf of Mexico to the upper Missouri. They were immigrants from the southwest, probably from the shores of the Gulf of California, and brought with them to their northern home some religious ceremonies and beliefs which remind us of the Aztecs. The usual form of sacrifice was a burnt offering. They lived in permanent villages, tilled the soil, and manufactured pottery. Some of their traditions allude to a time when a woman was their chief.

It is hoped that from the foregoing pages some notion may be had of the past and present condition of some of the best-known tribes of the North Americans.

INDEX.

269

THE END.

www.ingramcontent.com/pod-product-compliance
Lightning Source LLC
Chambersburg PA
CBHW031147270326
41931CB00006B/172